PUBLIC KNOWLEDGE, PRIVATE IGNORANCE

RECENT TITLES IN CONTRIBUTIONS IN LIBRARIANSHIP AND INFORMATION SCIENCE

Series Editor: PAUL WASSERMAN

Subject Retrieval in the Seventies: New Directions. An International Symposium
Hans (Hanan) Wellisch and Thomas D. Wilson, Editors

Quantitative Methods in Librarianship: Standards, Research, Management
Irene Braden Hoadley and Alice S. Clark, Editors

Public Relations for Libraries: Essays in Communications Techniques
Allan Angoff, Editor

Human Memory and Knowledge: A Systems Approach
Glynn Harmon

Libraries in the Political Scene
Marta L. Dosa

Information Retrieval and Documentation in Chemistry
Charles H. Davis and James E. Rush

Illustrative Computer Programming for Libraries: Selected Examples for Information Specialists
Charles H. Davis

University Science and Engineering Libraries: Their Operation, Collections, and Facilities
Ellis Mount

Participative Management in Academic Libraries
Maurice P. Marchant

Libraries As Communication Systems
J.M. Orr

A Community Elite and the Public Library: The Uses of Information in Leadership
Pauline Wilson

PUBLIC KNOWLEDGE, PRIVATE IGNORANCE

Toward a Library and Information Policy

PATRICK WILSON

*Contributions in Librarianship
and Information Science
Number 10*

GREENWOOD PRESS
Westport, Connecticut • London, England

Library of Congress Cataloging in Publication Data

Wilson, Patrick, 1927-
  Public knowledge, private ignorance.

  (Contributions in librarianship and information science ; no. 10)
  Includes bibliographical reference and index.
  1. Libraries. 2. Knowledge, Sociology of. 3. Information science. I. Title. II. Series.
Z665.W76   020   76-52327
ISBN 0-8371-9485-7

Library of Congress Catalog Card Number: 76-52327
ISBN 0-8371-9485-7

First published in 1977

Greenwood Press, Inc.
51 Riverside Avenue, Westport, Connecticut 06880

Printed in the United States of America

10 9 8 7 6 5 4 3 2

CONTENTS

PREFACE

What have libraries to do with the utilization of knowledge? What is, and what might be, their role in helping to make the results of inquiry useful in aiding the informed conduct of our lives? These are the principal questions to which this essay is addressed. The intent is practical: to help us understand better what would and what would not be sensible goals for the future of the nation's libraries. The task set here is not the formulation or evaluation of specific proposals, but rather the provision of a background against which specific proposals and policies can be better understood and more realistically evaluated. Any policy for library system development should be based on an understanding of the way in which what is known is represented in, and recoverable from, the documents that constitute the library's chief, though not sole, stock. The first chapter aims to aid that understanding. Any policy should be based on an understanding of individual information-gathering behavior. This requires more than statistics on the actual use made of libraries and other information sources; it requires a theory that explains and predicts behavior. The second chapter offers a theory that attempts to provide a framework for describing individual behavior and a means for explaining and predicting changes in behavior—all in terms not remote from our ordinary understanding of intelligent human action. Finally, any policy must be based on an understanding of what library use and library services are and might be like; some crucial aspects of these topics are discussed in the third chapter, in the light of the previous chapters. The discussion is not meant to be either complete or definitive.

Questions of technology, of financing, and of administration of library systems, for instance, receive no attention, and others of central importance to the evaluation of policy proposals, such as the problem of the measurement of worth or benefit, receive only glancing attention. Nor is this essay offered as the last word on any of the topics that are discussed. This is a contribution to a continuing inquiry and discussion that must go on among a wider audience than only those directly concerned with formulating policy proposals and planning future library systems and services. Everyone seriously concerned with libraries must care about understanding how knowledge is represented in documents, how people conduct their information-gathering activities, and how libraries do and can help to bring knowledge to bear where it is useful. For those are the central areas one has to investigate simply to understand the role of the library in the complex array of social arrangements for disseminating knowledge, as well as to decide for oneself what that role could and should be in the future.

ACKNOWLEDGMENTS

I am grateful to the following people for comments on a draft of this work: Michael K. Buckland, Michael D. Cooper, Mona Farid, Theodora Hodges, William Paisley, and Raynard C. Swank. As they will notice, I did not manage to heed all of their good advice. A seminar in information service policy given jointly with Howard D. White in 1974 prepared the way for parts of the third chapter. The research assistance of Mona Farid was especially valuable in parts of the second chapter. A small grant from the Committee on Research of the Academic Senate of the University of California, Berkeley, helped with incidental expenses. Finally, the glorious institution of the sabbatical leave gave me the time I needed to sort things out and write things down.

PUBLIC KNOWLEDGE, PRIVATE IGNORANCE

PUBLIC KNOWLEDGE

PUBLIC KNOWLEDGE AND
DOCUMENTARY RESEARCH

Scholars and scientists engage in attempts to make contributions to a public body of knowledge about the world. They do not work simply to increase their own private understanding of the world, nor simply to increase the understanding of their co-workers in a specialized branch of inquiry. Their work is incomplete until they have made their results public, available to anyone, now and in the future, who can understand and make use of them. Scholarly and scientific inquiry is a public enterprise, with a public goal, that of adding to or improving the public stock of knowledge.[1] Scholars and scientists are by no means the only ones who make contributions to the stock. Explorers and reporters, government officials and employees of business firms, lawyers and doctors, amateurs of cookery and cryptanalysis, in short, all who publish the results of their inquiries, observations, data collections or reminiscences may also make additions to the public stock of knowledge. Not everything that has been found out about the world and about how to work in the world has been made public: much remains untold and forgotten, some is kept secret, most autobiographies are never written, and much knowledge is unformulable and implicit, exhibited in practice but not reducible to verbal instructions. But much has been made public, in the form of durable published records, of which libraries are full.

The public stock of knowledge is not simply the sum of what is known by the separate individuals in the world; it is at once more and less than that. It is less, simply because much of what individuals know has not been, and never will be, made public. It is more, because much of what is known may be known *to* no one at all. A discovery made a hundred years ago, and preserved in the published records of inquiry, may still be a part of what is known about the world, even though no one now alive has ever examined the records in which it is preserved. "By a fiction as remarkable as any to be found in law, what has once been published, even though it be in the Russian language, is usually spoken of as 'known,' and it is often forgotten that the rediscovery in the library may be a more difficult and uncertain process than the first discovery in the laboratory."[2] It is odd to speak of things being known, though known to no one. But what makes it odd is not that the rediscovery in a library may be difficult; in that respect, knowledge existing only "in the literature" is no different from knowledge possessed by undiscoverable or inaccessible individuals. What makes it odd is rather the fact that what can be recorded is not knowledge, but only a representation of knowledge. If I write a message to myself, recording some fact that I fear I may forget, and do forget it, I can recover the knowledge by reference to my note, but the piece of paper does not know what I have forgotten. It bears a message, but it is not the bearer of knowledge. Where there is knowledge, there must be a knower; pieces of paper know nothing. This is what makes it a fiction to speak of knowledge that no one has. But it is a highly useful fiction. One can refer to the same phenomenon by speaking of virtual or potential knowledge in recorded form, but this alternate terminology avoids no difficulties and changes nothing. In either case, public knowledge includes much that is not known to anyone.

If the public stock of knowledge is not to be identified with the sum of what is known by individuals, still less is it to be identified with the sum of beliefs held by one or more individuals alive at any particular time or with the sum of things said in the collection of documents that has accumulated by a particular time. Our heads are full of nonsense, mistakes, wild conjectures, prejudices, and outmoded and superseded opinions; so are documents. The British scientist J. D. Bernal, writing in 1939, was of the opinion that perhaps three quarters of the scientific literature did not deserve to be published at all.[3] Thirty years later, a director of the United States National Bureau of Standards noted that his experience had led him to question whether, for physical data in general, the bulk of the published literature was really of any value.[4] Only a fraction of the things said in the documents belong to the body of public knowledge; to make things more complex still, some of the things that do belong to the body of knowledge are not things said in any of the documents explicitly, but are only implied by, or implicit in, those documents. The connection between the published records and the body of public knowledge is complex and indirect, as is the connection between individual beliefs and the body of knowledge.

Everyone has a more or less well-developed private view of the world, of what is in it and how it works. This is often referred to as an image or mental map of the world; it is better to think of it as a small-scale working model rather than a static picture or map, for it includes representations of how things behave over time, how they work, and how they change. Everyone's private view of the world differs from everyone else's, and the views that people actually do have are only a tiny few of the possible ones. Novelists draw pictures of imaginary views of the world held by imaginary people, and any of us could, if we wanted to, describe an imaginary view of the world in as much detail as we liked, a view that was "reasonable" (like our own) or "unreasonable" (drastically different from our own). We can also construct images of the world under various sorts of self-imposed limitation, constraint, or discipline, and public knowledge is best seen as a particular image invented under constraint. Its construction is based solely on what has been made public—on the public messages of private individuals. It is the best image constructible on this basis, the best view of the world attainable at a particular time on the basis of what people have said publicly. It has to be constructed, and construction must follow the principles and procedures for selection and rejection among alternative views of the world that are socially established at the time of construction. Public knowledge is, then, the view of the world that is the best we can construct at a given time, judged by our own best procedures for criticism and evaluation of the published record. Now the anomaly in the statement that something may be known but known *to* no one disappears, for what it means is simply that the thing said to be known would pass the current tests for inclusion in a representation of the best presently available view of the world.

This explanation of the concept of public knowledge is not meant as an explanation of the concept of knowledge. Paradoxically, much of what would count as public knowledge would not count as knowledge at all, at least on one well-known standard analysis of the concept of knowledge. According to the standard analysis, knowledge is at the very least true belief; knowledge implies truth, and where there is no belief, there is no knowledge. But we are allowing things to be part of public knowledge that are unknown to, and hence not believed by, anyone. And what is unmistakably part of public knowledge at a given time not only may turn out not to be true, but may even be strongly suspected at the time not to be true. When I want to find out what scientists have learned about, say, black holes, I will ask for the best presently available story—public knowledge—even though I may strongly suspect that this story will be replaced in the coming years by quite different stories. Looking back, I may say: that old story was far from the truth, but it was, nevertheless, the best story we then had. So public knowledge does not imply truth and, therefore, is not knowledge.

Having made this necessary point, we will henceforward ignore it, sticking to our concept of public knowledge but using the term *knowledge* casually and informally, forgetting the standard analysis. A skeptic might deny that we really have any knowledge at all (with heavy emphasis on the *really*); a surveyor of public knowledge might say that although the skeptic may well be right, he has to get on with his job, which is to discover the best presently available story about the world. That is the job that is of interest in this chapter—not the question of whether the best available story is in fact a true story.

The best available view of the world need not be complete, precise, or definite in every detail, any more than a private individual's view is. Like a map of an only partly explored territory, it will be blank in some areas, and sketchy in others. In some areas, only vague and indefinite views will be available; in others, ranges of equally plausible alternatives will be reported rather than a single established view. All gradations of credibility from tentative conjecture to certainty have to be represented; the degrees of uncertainty associated with different elements of public knowledge are an essential part of the picture, and the best presently available view of the world will exhibit a wide range of degrees of uncertainty. In this respect, the concept of public knowledge differs once again from at least one interpretation of the concept of knowledge. It is often useful to distinguish what we are certain of from what we suspect or believe but are not certain of; the term *knowledge* may be reserved for the former. That is not being done here, however; the notion of certainty has no dominant role in the theory of public knowledge. Public knowledge no more implies certainty than it implies truth. Indeed, we can comfortably get along without any certainty whatever; one who reports on a survey of an area of inquiry may begin by saying, "We are certain of nothing," but he need not end there.

Public knowledge has to be constructed, and we must presently review what we know of the process of construction. But first we should return to the question of making knowledge public. Making knowledge public does not imply success in getting people to notice what one makes public. No one may buy one's book or read one's journal article. But publishing is taking the first step in sending a message through the world. What is unread has no contemporary influence and does not change anyone's mind, but it may nevertheless be, or contain, a contribution to public knowledge that will be discovered at a later time. The scientist who publishes his results presumably wants to influence his colleagues and make a contribution to knowledge. If his work is unread, the first aim is not attained, but the second may still be.[5]

There are more ways of making something public than simply publishing books and articles. The scientific finding reported orally at an open meeting has been made public. What we have told our friends and are prepared to tell anyone who asks, we have made public. So what has been published is only a fraction of what has been made public. If scientific and scholarly research is the source of much of what is in our fund of public knowledge and is more or less completely represented by published documents, still it cannot be seriously claimed that everything that is known is the result of scientific and scholarly research; science and public knowledge are not the same.[6] Innumerable facts of ordinary social life, of geography and natural history, of human procedures and technology are publicly available, though perhaps not recorded. A view of the world based only on published documents would leave out too much of what is known of the world.

To this objection there is a ready answer. A systematic survey of all public knowledge would require a huge preliminary job of transcription, putting into writing what has been made public but is not in written form, recording what is widely known, and eliciting what people are prepared to tell anyone who asks. Much private knowledge would incidentally become public in this process; the boundary between public and private is often purely accidental, and what has hitherto been private will be made public on the slightest provocation. Whatever can be transcribed, then, even if it has not yet been transcribed, is potentially raw material for the construction of public knowledge.

But this answer raises another problem, for there may be much that is known, but cannot be captured in any transcription. It is widely doubted that we can completely specify our technology in the form of sets of instructions; there is much we know how to do that we cannot say how to do. For much of our practical knowledge, it seems that all we can do is provide exhibitions or performances; in particular, we cannot provide instructions for performance that are complete enough to allow another to develop the ability to carry out similar performances by following the instructions. Complex skills are learned, not from following manuals of instruction, but by practice under criticism and coaching. We learn by doing, or trying to do, not by following explicit instructions. And so any representation of practical knowledge in verbal form must be an inadequate representation, if a verbal form is discoverable at all.

If it is true that one often cannot acquire practical knowledge simply by reading and trying to follow a set of instructions, it is equally true that one often cannot acquire theoretical knowledge simply by reading and trying to follow an exposition. If I simply cannot grasp the sense of what I read, then I acquire no knowledge by the reading I do. I may learn by heart a sentence that expresses something others know; until I understand its meaning, what it expresses is not anything I can be said to know. What I do not understand, I cannot be said to know. I show that I understand something I have read by the variety of things I am able to do on the basis of what I have read: draw inferences, paraphrase, recognize applications and instances, calculate in new ways, act appropriately in a new range of situations. Knowledge is tested in the same way, not by parrot-like repetition of sentences but by the exhibition of an ability to carry out the above variety of performances. Acquisition of knowledge is more than simply the acquisition of an understanding of a new statement or story, and the tests for knowledge must be more extensive than the tests for understanding. But the crucial point is that the former include the latter; the differences are irrelevant here. Having knowledge, like having understanding, is shown by the exhibition of an ability to perform a wide variety of verbal and nonverbal actions. We can even go on to identify the test with what is tested; if a person has the abilities expected of one who understands, what further evidence do we need to conclude that he understands? The understanding one acquires is the ability one develops, and the knowledge one acquires, whatever more it is, is at least the ability one acquires.

Both the acquisition of theoretical knowledge and the acquisition of practical knowledge are, then, the development of abilities. In all cases of public knowledge, both practical and theoretical, what can be made available to us is only some representation or exhibition of knowledge— a set of instructions, a statement, a performance. In all cases, acquiring knowledge involves more than coming to have in one's possession a representation of knowledge; it involves the development of an ability. There are never any guarantees that inspection of a particular representation of knowledge will lead to the development of the corresponding ability. One may lack the necessary capacity or talent, or the representation may simply be an ineffective one for a particular individual. Practical knowledge is not qualitatively different from theoretical knowledge in respect to its communicability, that is, the ease with which the knowledge can be acquired by others on the basis of representations or exhibitions of it. So while it may be true that much that is known cannot be captured in any transcription, the force of this is not that there are things known that cannot be told, but rather that any particular attempt to tell them may fail to produce knowledge in others. But an attempt that fails for one person may succeed with another. I may fail to make flakey pie crust when attempting to follow your instructions, but others may succeed; I may fail to grasp your theory or follow your argument, but another may succeed. The substance of the claim that we have knowledge that cannot be captured in transcription is that we cannot invariably provide algorithms—completely specific instructions that invariably lead to successful performance—for performances, and that we cannot invariably provide foolproof explanations. This does not mean that we cannot, therefore, make such knowledge public; it simply means that making it public will not always allow others to acquire it. But public knowledge does not have to be successfully communicable in that sense. It has already been noted that making knowledge public does not guarantee that anyone will notice it; now it has to be added that making knowledge public does not guarantee that anyone will understand, or develop the operational ability that they would have to develop in order to acquire the knowledge themselves. If we required of public knowledge that it be made public in a form intelligible to everyone, we would limit it to what is available to the most limited intelligence. But if we allow that representations of public knowledge may not be invariably successful vehicles through which others can come to share what is represented, then there is no good reason to draw the line at one degree of imperfection in communication rather than another. Whatever can be represented at all is, then, a candidate for public knowledge—and that is surely all the knowledge that one would ever care to count in the public stock.

The public stock of knowledge changes constantly, as the stock of published records grows. Not every newly published document changes the stock of knowledge; those that do may change it in other ways than by the simple addition of new bits of knowledge. To discover the extent of change in the body of knowledge, we have perpetually to review the results of inquiry, and make new accounts and new representations of what it is that we can say we know about the world.[7] We have again and again to survey the state of knowledge, or the state of the different arts (where knowledge is practical rather than theoretical). This is work that involves more than simple inspection, spotting sheep and eliminating goats. It is a job of construction. Let us see what the job is like. The task is not, or not primarily, to increase our knowledge, but simply to say what it is. It is, then, not a job of original research, but it is a job of research: library research, or, as we shall call it, documentary research. The first part of the job is to locate and assemble the relevant literature; this is a bibliographical task and by no means always an easy or straightforward one. The next job is to analyze and evaluate the pieces of literature found. This is a twofold task, of internal criticism, to determine whether what is said is convincingly supported within the document, and of external criticism, to determine whether what is said is consistent with what other documents report, and to determine in general how it relates to other documents. The result of internal and external criticism might range from outright rejection of a document as of no value at all, to total acceptance without qualifications.

The result of internal and external criticism of a collection of separate documents would not, however, be more than the beginning of the work. For the next question would be: what can we say, on the basis of the documents thus evaluated? And what we *can* say need not be what *is* said in any of the documents. It is possible to imagine surveys in which each work surveyed was exclusively devoted to the establishment of a single fact independent of every other fact, so that the final summary would be simply the rehearsal of the separate facts found to be sufficiently established by the separate investigations. But this is not the general case. To suppose it was would be to suppose that the process of science and scholarship did indeed resemble the accumulation of a sand-heap of discrete facts accumulated by investigators working in logical and actual isolation from each other, a view that never was reasonable and by now is quite incredible. What any particular investigation can be claimed to show need not be what its author claimed to show; the conclusions that are justifiable or allowable on the basis of the work done and the evidence presented may be weaker or stronger than claimed by the author. And what the cumulative effort of a group of investigators together shows may not be what any of them individually saw or claimed. This is obvious enough if we think of separate investigations of examples or species of a common genus: generalizations allowable by the whole group of investigations might not be allowable by, or made in the course of, any of the independent inquiries. But straight generalization from a family of examples is only one, and the least interesting, of the possibilities. A story that appears out of a number of independent inquiries, a theory incidentally confirmed by remote and tangential inquiries, another theory incidentally discredited, all may be the cumulative effect of independent inquiries. Negative conclusions are as possible as positive: a number of inquiries might show such a range of weaknesses and defects, and might be mutually inconsistent in so many respects, that the conclusion must be that nothing has been shown. Mixed verdicts may be given: the literature yields some support for each of several inconsistent theories, no one of which can be held to have been either confirmed or refuted, all still occupying a place in the field of live possibilities.

The striking thing about the process of evaluation of a body of work is that, while the intent is not to increase knowledge by the conducting of independent inquiries, the result may be the increase of knowledge, by the drawing of conclusions not made in the literature reviewed but supported by the part of it judged valid.[8] The process of analysis and synthesis can produce new knowledge in just this sense, that the attempt to put down what can be said to be known, on the basis of a given collection of documents, may result in the establishment of things not claimed explicitly in any of the documents surveyed. What results from such a survey may at no point be identical with what is said in the texts surveyed. So far from the survey's being a simple collection of true sentences out of a body of texts, it may be a presentation that differs in every particular from the contents of the work surveyed.

In these characteristics, the work of the surveyor of public knowledge resembles that of the historian. Both work with documents, both are concerned to say what we can claim to know on the basis of the documents. (Of course, the historian has other sources, too.) In neither case is the work confined to the extraction of snippets from the source documents; in both cases, external and internal criticism of individual documents is a prelude to the creation of a coherent story that may say things that are said in none of the source documents. It is evident that the historian's story does not arise automatically from the colligation of independent source documents, even after the process of criticism. The historian must construct his story, on the basis of the sources; and this is an act of invention. The reviewer of the state of knowledge is in an analogous position. For him, too, the story does not arise automatically from the evaluated documents; it is, or may well be, an invention, a creation. Just as the historian's invention must be justifiable on the basis of the sources, so must the reviewer's; invention is under the control of the sources. But the reviewer is no more limited to putting down extracts than is the historian. As there are more and less creative, constructive, ambitious histories, so there are more and less creative, constructive, ambitious critical reviews of knowledge. It is true that much of what goes under the name of reviews of knowledge or of the progress of research is almost wholly uncritical, mere collections of uncritical remarks on separate reports of inquiry; this is hack work. But good reviews are not like this. We shall not understand the process of reviewing knowledge at all, unless we think of it as capable of more than banal reports of what people think they have discovered.

The comparison with the work of an historian suggests that in the process of surveying the achievements of a field, different surveyors might well arrive at different results. This is obviously true if we allow that new results may appear in the course of a survey; unless the new results emerge mechanically from the analysis of old work, their emergence depends on the surveyor's imagination or inventiveness—controlled, to be sure, by the basic sources as well as his own critical judgment. Even if we put aside the question of the discovery or invention of new things and consider only the evaluation of old things, is there any reason to suppose that different surveyors, even equally competent and judicious surveyors, will arrive at the same results? Surely not; the process described above is not mechanical, determined in every particular by explicit rules, and inevitably leading to a single result. Different surveyors of the same area may produce slightly

or widely different results; what one says has been established, another
may say is no better than a tentative hypothesis; what one notices as
implied, another may not notice at all. This is the more likely, the more
one tries to survey knowledge in the light of its bearing on action and
policies for action.[9] As long as the surveyor can limit himself to enumer-
ating the uncontroversial, firmly established findings of the field surveyed,
the possibility of different and incompatible surveys of the same field is
not a very live one. But if the surveyor tries to do more than simply summarize the uncontroversial, if he tries to squeeze from a group's results
as much as possible that bears on a practical problem, then the possibility
of sharp conflict between different surveys becomes live, indeed. We are
not talking about conflicting advice and conflicting recommendations;
these certainly are common but are not what concern us here. The con-
flicts of concern are those over what the state of knowledge is: over what
we are entitled to say we have found out, or what we should treat as having
been found out, for purposes of action. The very cautious surveyor might
refuse to go beyond what was established beyond all doubt, but then action
and policy might be given no guidance at all, for what is established may
not be what is needed, and what is needed may not have been finally
established. Action cannot wait for final establishment; we have to go on
the basis of the best information we have, however far from certain it
may be. And when surveyors try to say what *is* the best information we
have, they may and frequently do come to very different conclusions.
This poses a familiar problem for those who wish to get guidance on what
to do. How can I know what is known about a subject if I am given different
and conflicting stories? Even if I am given only a single story, how can I
know whether it is trustworthy? We cannot, it will turn out, satisfactorily
answer these questions, for there are no satisfactory answers. But we can
go a certain way. To go even a short way, we have to turn to a discussion
of the social organization of inquiry.

SPECIALISTS IN KNOWLEDGE

The cultivation of knowledge is the assigned social responsibility of a
number of distinct occupational groups; what was once left to individual
amateurs has become organized and incorporated into the social division
of labor. Common sense reflects what are by now basic social arrangements

when it tells us that, if you want to know about meteorology or statistics, you should ask a meteorologist or a statistician. Others may know some or much of what these people know; but if one is uncertain which other people know much about the subject, one would settle the question by appeal to the "specialists." Statistician and meteorologist are occupational categories; they indicate work that consists in, or essentially involves, the discovery of knowledge. They are "knowledge occupations," and it is a basic principle about public knowledge that those whose occupation it is to cultivate a field of knowledge are those who are in a position to say what, in particular, the field has yielded.[10] They not only try to find more knowledge, they also have to say what has so far been found. But they are not in a position to say whether the field yields any knowledge at all; that question is too important to be left to them and is instead socially answered, by the recognition of the field as a knowledge-producing field or the contrary.

One of the hallmarks of a profession, such as medicine or law, is its claim to an exclusive right to practice a certain art, and the social recognition of an occupation as a profession involves recognition of this right. The same claim is made by knowledge-producing groups; in their case, it is the claim to the possession of the best techniques for discovering new things and of the best procedures for deciding what has been discovered. The latter is more basic than the former, for it need not be claimed that no one outside the occupational group and using other techniques could ever discover anything in their area of specialization; as long as they have the last word on what, if anything, the outsider has discovered, they need not claim that no other techniques than their own can possibly yield results. This is obviously so for the social sciences, many, if not all, of whose objects of investigation are the things of ordinary life with which we are all acquainted. There, surprises are not frequent, and confirmation or refutation of the results of unspecialized commonsense observation is a major task. But the claim to possess superior techniques for the discovery of new things, and for the more exact and accurate determination of what can roughly and approximately be gathered by unspecialized inquiry, is nevertheless essential, for unless it is granted that they do indeed have ways of discovering new things, they are at best a group of censors, not a group of contributors. Both parts of the claim are granted for many occupational groups. Most nonscientists have only the sketchiest notion of how scientists work, but they are, by and large, prepared to grant that, whatever the procedures are, they yield knowledge, and that, if others outside the occupational group claim to have made discoveries within the area claimed by a specialist group of scientists, the insiders are the ones to determine whether the discoveries are real or not.[11] It is just such a concession that establishes an occupation as a contributor to the body of public knowledge.

It is often convenient to distinguish professions from academic disciplines; this is customary in universities. But doing so tends to conceal the professional character of the established academic disciplines.[12] Members of professional groups offer services—advice or action, or both—presumably based on specialized knowledge. Members of the academic disciplines offer services, too, namely, teaching, consulting, and advising. Members of the academic disciplines conduct research, more or less, but members of the professions are not precluded from trying to discover new knowledge, and many manage to do so. Economists and physicists advise governments, doctors of medicine conduct research, doctors and engineers discover new technology. They all *profess,* as Everett Hughes reminds us: they profess to know better than other people the nature of certain matters.[13] The mix of different activities is different from one group to another and within groups; discovery of new things is more important in some, and converting general knowledge into judgment on what to do in a particular case is more important in others. But the established professions and the established academic disciplines have established themselves in the same way, by securing a grant of exclusive jurisdiction over some area of specialized knowledge. Both have techniques or methods they claim to be best for working their areas, and both claim the right to decide what is good work in their areas. Relatively few people are exclusively engaged in research, the systematic attempt to discover new knowledge; college professors are at least expected to be teachers as well as researchers, and most of them are primarily teachers.[14] We must not expect to find a sharp line drawn between those occupations that are exclusively and entirely knowledge-producing and all the others, or suppose that "all the others" are wholly disengaged from such work. Only academic snobbishness would explain the view that the academic disciplines and well-entrenched professions were the only occupations in which there was any significant amount of knowledge acquired for the first time and used as the basis of performance. Mankind was accumulating knowledge long before the professions were established, and now that they are established, they have no monopoly on the discovery of new things. But it is still true that a relatively few occupations are preeminently devoted to the cultivation of knowledge and are socially recognized as being so.

The social grant of authority and responsibility for the cultivation of an area of investigation implies a belief that there is something to investigate and that the group given authority has effective procedures for investigation. If we do not believe in the phenomena of, say, extrasensory perception, we will not recognize the claims of the students of those phenomena to jurisdiction over the area, for there is nothing in the area. If we recognize the existence of objects of investigation but are unconvinced that the claimant group actually has an effective means of investigation, we will not recognize its claims; we can, for instance, admit that the future is indeed an object for investigation, without admitting the efficacy of new techniques for foretelling the future. Also, a social grant of exclusive jurisdiction once given may later be withdrawn, what was once accepted as a real knowledge-producing field, with real objects to investigate and real methods for investigation, being finally rejected, due to the growth of disbelief in either the objects or the methods, or both. Once a group has been established, it has authority to say what in particular it has learned; over the specifics of its findings, society retains no authority. But rejection in toto of the field's "discoveries" remains possible; what was once established can be disestablished. It would no doubt strike a member of an established, entrenched knowledge occupation, such as chemistry, as absurd to argue that whether his group contributes to public knowledge depends on whether society grants, and continues to grant, recognition to his group. But students of extrasensory perception and foretellers of the future may be quite as confident as any chemist. It is not enough, in order to be a contributor to public knowledge, to think one is; the rest of us have got to think so, too.[15]

The social recognition of an occupational group as a knowledge-producing profession need not be a sudden or definitely recognizable event, though there are events that are signs of the acquisition of status—for example, the creation of departments of instruction in universities, the award of research grants by governments, and the appointment of official advisers to governments.[16] The acquisition and the loss of recognition may be gradual, and at any particular time a number of occupational groups may be uncomfortably somewhere between establishment and disestablishment. If their status is indefinite, so is the corresponding question of whether their current views form part of public knowledge. With reference to the current views of established groups, the surveyor of public knowledge can say simply, "It is known that . . . " or, "We know that . . . "; with reference to those whose status is in doubt, he can only report, "It is held that . . .," or, "One groups asserts that . . . ." Social recognition of a group is the process that converts private belief into public knowledge.

A survey of knowledge falls under the jurisdiction of the appropriate occupational group; it is their job to do such surveys, for it is their job not only to find out new things but to say what has so far been found out in their area of responsibility. The surveyor must be, or be prepared to become, a specialist in the subject matter being surveyed, and ordinarily this means that he must be a member of the group whose work is being surveyed.[17] One would not ask a literary critic to review the findings of molecular biology or of classical archaeology. This is not to say that outsiders to a group are forbidden to try to summarize the group's findings. Judgment can be exercised by anyone. A cat can look at a queen and not like what it sees. But if it is the group that has final say over the accuracy of surveys, the group will not even take seriously the survey done by one lacking what they consider the most elementary qualifications. No one will be allowed competent to judge who is not competent to practice in the field being judged. Outsiders show their consent to this view, which is just a facet of the professional status granted to the group, by their preference, whenever the need for a survey arises, for one done by a "recognized expert," or an "established authority in the field." Anyone else may try, and an amateur might do what was recognized by the group as a surprisingly good job. But the group would claim the right to the last word.

There are perfectly good reasons for the requirement that the surveyor be also a member of the group being surveyed. For how can one attain the requisite understanding of the field except by going through the initiation customary for entrants into the field (graduate study, a dissertation, etc.)? It *can* be done, but by a process of self-education equivalent to the standard initiation. Let us consider a field of inquiry that is not socially established as contributing to knowledge at all—an esoteric theology, for instance. It is easy to imagine that an unestablished theology may have ways, perhaps shared by no one else, of sorting out reasonable from unreasonable, plausible from implausible, and convincing from unconvincing arguments and claims. There may be an answer to the question of what is the best current view of the field's findings, in terms of the procedures accepted in the field, even when outsiders deny that the best current view has any truth to it at all. But the outsider could not answer that question without transporting himself to the inside, not merely to the degree that he could understand what was said, but to the degree that he could operate as the insiders operate on their material. He might do this under a lengthy suspension of disbelief, but he would have to be the working equivalent of a theologian himself before he could be considered a trustworthy reporter on the current state of their (pseudo) science. The difference between this situation and that of a "true" field of knowledge is irrelevant from the point of view of the question: Who is competent to judge the state of knowledge in the field?

There are important exceptions to the general rule that a competent surveyor must first be a competent practitioner. Every field of inquiry employs methods and tools of inquiry that are common to other fields of inquiry, as well as some that are particular to itself. At the very least, every field of inquiry that is now socially established must use, or claim to use, the common human tool of rational argument; it must draw conclusions from premises according to generally valid rules. After "common logic", mathematics is the most nearly universally used tool. It is apparent, simply by reference to these familiar tools, that valid criticism from the outside is possible, and that the group's claim to be in charge of saying what it has found is hedged around with protective exceptions and limits to the extent of its authority. The outsider may be able to see that a field's use of these common tools is faulty; even without understanding all of the group's inarticulate assumptions and standards, it may be evident that their logic is poor and their computations wrong. Insofar as a group uses, in its work, tools of inquiry that are common to other groups, its work can be appraised by the outsider who is master of the tools. But mastery is demonstrated within *some* professional group, and the rule that the surveyor must be a competent practitioner is still in force; the outsider can survey the group's work to the extent that it depends on tools of which he is master. Presumably it is by this shared use of tools of inquiry, with its concomitant overlapping of procedures, interest, and subject matter among different fields, that distinct occupational groups are subject to a sort of social control by outsiders.[18]

It is by no means excluded from this account that, given the position of the occupational specialists, we may also recognize particular individuals as deserving the same authority as a surveyor of knowledge, though they are not members of the specialist group. That a particularly gifted person knows more about a subject than most of its specialists can be admitted while recognizing the primacy of the work group. But if we thought all outsiders knew more than the specialists, the specialists would have no status at all as managers of a field of knowledge. It also remains true that, if I start out looking for someone who can tell me what is known in a particular field, it would be considered plainly irrational of me to prefer someone who was not a member of the appropriate occupational group over a member, unless I had independent reasons for thinking the outsider more knowledgeable than most of the insiders. In an important sense of the term *organization,* knowledge is organized in terms of occupational groups; the distribution of knowledge, and of knowledge about knowledge, corresponds closely to the organization of occupational specialties. We can recognize gifted amateurs and polymaths who are masters of many specialties as easily as we can admit the existence of incompetent specialists. But if we suspect a whole group of incompetence and always prefer the views of the outsider to those of the insider, then we have, at least in our own case, disestablished the field, for we have come to disbelieve that these people, proceeding as they do, can provide any reliable results. As with the making of new discoveries, so with saying what the past effort has yielded. It is not an accidental fact that we think the occupational specialists to be in a special position to say what their field has discovered; it follows from the fact of establishment that the specialists are in that position.

To say that the occupational specialists are in a special position to judge what their field has discovered is not to say how they do the judging. We grant the claims of knowledge-producing groups without knowing how they do their work, and we also grant it without knowing how they decide or discover what they have discovered. One might suppose each group to have explicit and complete rules for evaluation and criticism of different claims to discovery, rules established and accepted by all the members of the group. The group's contribution to public knowledge would then be the corpus of statements implicitly or explicitly picked out of their published writings by the rules, as acceptable at a given time, and there would be an objective test for the accuracy of surveys of the knowledge gained in their field.[19] But no science or systematic branch of inquiry has such rules (though mathematics may come close).[20] Going to the other extreme and abandoning any reference to rules for evaluation and criticism, one might suppose that what the members of a specialty can be said to have discovered depends simply on what some particular community thinks they have discovered. We have already implicitly rejected one version of that thesis, according to which the relevant community is the whole population of occupational specialists in knowledge, and public knowledge is what commands universal assent in that community.[21] But it is wholly implausible to suppose that what the physicists can be said to have discovered depends on what botanists and psychologists think physicists have discovered; and if we found that those who were responsible both for discovering new knowledge and for deciding what knowledge had so far been gained did so without regard to any shared standards of criticism, we would be likely to take back the social grant of authority given them.

We shall then continue to assume that each specialist group determines what are its own findings, on the basis of shared, though incomplete and not explicitly formulated, standards of evaluation. But we still do not know how such groups decide, if indeed they can be said to decide, what they have so far found out. Some writers, pointing to the unequal distribution of prestige and authority in scientific groups, have claimed that the most influential members of the group decide (though not formally) what the group has discovered; the views of the "foremost authorities in the field" determine the current state of knowledge.[22] If this were so, we could think of these "authorities" as constituting a congress or parliament, the group's contribution to public knowledge depending, not necessarily on what that congress decides, but on what it would decide if forced to choose. But we can just as easily imagine a direct democracy, with each properly enfranchised member of the group having an equal vote. No doubt it sounds strange to talk of voting in this context, but formal organizations of scientists and scholars can and do formally endorse, approve, authorize statements of all sorts; why should they not endorse surveys of public knowledge, and why not by voting?[23] In the case of either representative (if the "authorities" can indeed be said to represent others) or direct democracy, the same question would arise: how many must agree for a description of the group's findings to be accepted as correct? Unanimity seems too strong a requirement; it is implausible to suppose that one stubbornly unconvinced member could forestall a group decision. A simple majority is too weak a requirement; if only 50 percent plus one of a group of investigators hold one view, the rest holding another, we would think the group badly divided and lacking a consensus. (To speak of consensus, however, simply raises the question: How much agreement constitutes consensus?) Perhaps the best suggestion is that near-unanimity, in the light of generally shared standards of evaluation and representing the decision that would be arrived at if the matter were put to a vote, is required for approval of a description of a group's findings as correct.

But this does not tell us about the state of public knowledge when there is conflict within a group, when, for instance, competing surveys of knowledge would divide the members of the group into opposing factions. Nor does it suggest any way of assuring ourselves that a given survey is the best that could be produced. When an overt conflict arises between different surveyors of knowledge, we have to say that, so long as the conflict is unresolved, the status of public knowledge is simply indeterminate in the area of conflict. Even when there is no conflict and, in fact, no competition at all between different versions of what the state of knowledge is, we do not know that the accepted survey is the best survey. The members of the relevant group can themselves only judge among alternatives that are given to them; they could themselves have no basis for saying that a particular survey was the best job that could possibly be done. How could they know that? Even if they all set themselves to work trying to improve on a given survey and failed, nothing would have been shown except that it was not easy to improve on the surveyor's work. So there is a sense in which we can never be sure that we know what is known— not the usual sense that we cannot be sure which of the things we now believe will still be believable in the future, but a different and quite odd sense that we are not and cannot be sure of the present state of our own public view of the world. Attempts to say what we know are attempts at faithful representation of the best presently available view of the world, but we cannot get at that ideal best presently available view to compare it directly with a particular attempted representation, and we cannot be certain that the representation is a faithful one.

PARTICULAR QUESTIONS

We have been considering the problem of reviewing a collection of documents to determine what, on the basis of those documents, we can claim to know. Let us now turn to another sort of task, that in which we try to discover the best current answer to some particular question: For example, what is the present best estimate of the speed of light? On what is the best current view of the etiology of schizophrenia? These are equivalent to questions about public knowledge; they are of the form: What is the state of public knowledge with respect to this particular point? It is clear enough that, if the task is not simply to discover what someone else of appropriate critical qualifications has concluded was the state of public knowledge on the matter, but to see for oneself what the state of public knowledge is, then the task requires the same procedures and qualifications as does that of surveying a collection of documents to see what, in general, they show. Anyone who could perform the more general task could perform the more restricted task of finding what public knowledge was on a particular question. More important, one who could perform the restricted task could perform the more general task. This takes some showing.

Let us simplify matters by supposing that there is at least one explicit statement in the documents surveyed that constitutes an answer to the question posed, some explicit statement about the best present estimate of the speed of light, or the etiology of schizophrenia. If determination of the state of public knowledge on a particular matter were simply the discovery of some explicit answer to a question, or the discovery of the most recent statement if several have been made, then it would be hard to argue our point. One might discover such a statement even if one could barely, if at all, understand the statement. But such a view of the problem is impossible. The statement found might be entirely inconsistent with the rest of the body of public knowledge in the field; it might be unsupported by the evidence presented for it in its own context. But to assure oneself that its own context did constitute good support for the claim would be exactly to criticize the work internally by application of whatever standards were appropriate to the work, and to assure oneself that it was consistent with the rest of the body of public knowledge in the field would require that one be able, at least, to determine what that was; these tasks require the general ability already described.

If a statement found in a body of literature *may not* represent public knowledge, it is also, and already, clear that a statement nowhere found in a body of literature *may* represent public knowledge. The answer to a particular question may be part of the best image of the world constructible from a collection of documents, though it is not found in any of the documents. It may be "found" only by being invented. It may be part of public knowledge even though not included in any explicit survey of public knowledge so far made, for any survey will answer only the questions the surveyor thinks to ask, and no one manages to anticipate all the possible questions to which answers may be derivable from a collection of documents.

What of the question whether a survey done in the past is still a faithful description of what is known? To assert of an old survey that it is still valid amounts to the claim that documentary research, if conducted now, would find no revisions necessary in the light of subsequent publications, that there is no later evidence or findings that would require revision. It seems clear that no one could claim to be able to make such a judgment who was not competent to conduct a new survey himself. This is the meaning of the professional demand to be judged by one's peers: only those capable of doing this sort of work themselves are capable of telling whether this work has been well done or whether what was well done now requires revision. This does not mean that one can judge the past or present accuracy of a survey only if one could have produced that very survey; insofar as synthesis involves invention, which people are not equally good at, one may claim competence to judge what one could not have produced. But the critic who lacks capacity to perform the analytical part of the surveyor's task can claim no serious attention whatever. If the surveyor of a field must in general be a practitioner in the field, so must one who undertakes to answer particular questions within the scope of the field and to evaluate the past or present fidelity of a survey.

The tasks of saying what is known about some aspect of the world, of answering minute particular questions about public knowledge, and of saying that a new survey is accurate or an old survey still accurate, all call for the same qualifications: those of the practitioner in the field that is responsible for the particular area of knowledge. The outsider is always free to assert his own judgment and to disagree with the insiders, and if enough outsiders disagree with the insiders, the insiders may lose their position as recognized producers of knowledge. But as long as the group retains its socially granted authority, those who recognize this authority will accept no other judgment as having weight, unless it is the judgment of a representative of a group having a more firmly established grant of authority.

REFERENCE WORKS

What is an encyclopedia, asks Jacques Barzun, but a public repository of public knowledge?[24] If we could have a complete written representation of public knowledge, it would be the ultimate encyclopedia, the ultimate reference work. No one person could write it, and no one book could contain it. This is obvious, but is it obvious just how large it would be? Its size can be appreciated if we reflect that it would contain, as subparts, everything ever published. (The medieval encyclopedias that included the texts of ancient authors were on the right track.) Consider only telephone directories, a particularly useful and ubiquitous species of reference work. All of them would have to be included, and on two different grounds. First, all of them represent public knowledge, more or less—the knowledge that, at the time of issue, such and such parties had telephones with such numbers. Second, even if they had all been incorrect at the time of issue, it is still public knowledge that they *said* that such parties had such telephone numbers. Publication is an event, and one way (of course, not the only way) of describing the event is to quote the published text in full. Having said earlier that not every publication makes a contribution to public knowledge, we must now correct that statement. What is asserted in a writing may be false or meaningless and so no contribution to knowledge of its ostensible subject matter, but at least we know *that* these things were said. A document may not make the sort of contribution to public knowledge that its author hoped for, but it cannot fail to make some contribution, namely, to the history of talk. The complete encyclopedia, then, would replace all of our libraries because it would contain the contents of a complete library.

This would be only part of its contents; the rest would be the result of construction, on the basis of documentary research, of the most complete representation of the best view of the world attainable on the basis of the texts in that complete library. Evidently, the complete encyclopedia could not be written. This is so for many reasons. First, the necessary army of compilers would not, however great their ingenuity, exhaust the possibilities of analysis and synthesis of the records already published. Second, they could not be sure they had exhausted the records, even if they had exhausted their own ingenuity; the drive for completeness would require replacement of worn-out compilers by fresh workers. Third, the stock of records would continue to grow while the job of analysis and synthesis was under way, and every new addition to the stock would open the possibility of reconsidering all the work done so far, not only in the immediate area of the new contribution, but in all the neighboring and more remote areas that, by implication, might be affected. Fourth, and a generalization of the third point, a truly encyclopedic representation of public knowledge could not be a simple sum of separate contributions by "chapter editors" but would have to be as well the result of an analysis of the bearing of each part on every other part, and a mutual adjustment and correction of each in the light of all the rest. Unless this was done, the whole might be at worst a mass of inconsistencies, or at best a lost opportunity to strengthen and illumine parts by drawing on other parts; it would not be the best attainable picture of the world and so not an accurate representation of public knowledge. It is not clear who would be capable of the staggering synthesis required. The social organization of inquiry provides for people learned in this or that special branch of inquiry, but not for people especially good at adjudicating the claims of one field in the light of those of all of the others. It is not that the separate specialties work in isolation. They borrow from one another freely and criticize one another still more freely. But the borrowings are opportunistic, and the criticisms spasmodic and partial. As the records of work in one field are unlikely to be completely mined out, so the job of drawing the implications of knowledge in one field for knowledge in all others is unlikely to be completed. It's unlikely the job would be completed even if the stock of knowledge available in the separate fields were not changing so rapidly as in fact it is.

But finally, with respect to the conclusions reached at any time, the job of representing those conclusions in written form could never be finished, not for lack of wit or patience, but from the nature of the case. For the knowledge that is to be represented exists in the form of an ability to do things: to solve novel problems, answer novel questions, construct and evaluate novel chains of argument, detect the plausibility or implausibility of new claims, and make applications to new problems. A complete description of that ability would require complete specification of all those problems, questions, arguments, and so on. But that is plainly out of the question. If we had thought that we might construct an encyclopedia that fully represented public knowledge, we now see that the job is impossible.

Complete representation of public knowledge is impossible, but there is no particular point at which we would have to stop in our attempts to say what we know. In view of our preceding discussions, however, it is clear that two kinds of uncertainties are bound to plague our attempts to evaluate our success. First, there can be no guarantee that any survey or any part of the whole survey is the best one attainable at a given time. Second, the social status of different fields of inquiry may be indeterminate; there may be no social consensus on the question of which fields of inquiry are indeed contributors to public knowledge and hence deserving of representation in the great encyclopedia. The editors of the great encyclopedia could not escape problems of choice arising from the dependence of public knowledge on the social process of the establishment of fields as contributors to public knowledge, and from its character as a work of construction rather than simple description of given and uncontested results. The editors' problems of choice would be the judges' problems of evaluation. Have the right fields been included and excluded? Are the surveys indeed the best attainable? Again the old paradox appears: we cannot be quite certain that we know what we know.

We have already argued that the nonspecialist or the amateur is not in a position to evaluate surveys of knowledge, but the great encyclopedia, the public repository of public knowledge, once approved by the cognizant specialists, would be a means of making that knowledge available to everyone. But we must wonder what that means. Does it mean that any of us could come to have all the knowledge represented in the encyclopedia? Evidently not; having a representation of knowledge, we said earlier, is far from having knowledge. Acquiring knowledge is acquiring understanding, and only those who can understand what is said in the encyclopedia can be said to acquire the knowledge it represents. But this commonly depends on what one already knows: what is quickly and easily grasped by one with a certain sort of prior learning is slowly and laboriously grasped, or not grasped at all, by those without comparable learning. In the hands of the learned, the great encyclopedia would be nearly an aide-mémoire, the external memory often spoken of; for the unlearned, it would be no such thing.[25] The contrast between the availability and the accessibility of knowledge will concern us crucially at a later stage of our discussion.

It is clear enough that the necessary incompleteness in a representation of public knowledge is no serious practical inconvenience; we do not in fact seek completeness when we set about summarizing our knowledge. We have dwelt on the inevitable incompleteness of this imaginary encyclopedia, not to point out practical problems, but to elucidate further the character of public knowledge and the process of making it explicit.

Most of the things known are of too little interest for us to want to collect and organize them into reference works. Reports of scientific and scholarly research always omit masses of inconsequential detail that could have been included, and when the time comes for their compaction into a systematic survey, nothing may survive except a sentence or a number. Only what is of likely future interest is retained; things worth saying the first time need not be worth repeating forever in works of reference. The point of making reference works is to replace a large body of literature by a very much smaller body, containing only what is most worth repeating. (This does not, of course, apply to telephone directories!) And the criteria of worth are much the same in deciding what bears repeating as in deciding what is worth finding out in the first place: value depends on usefulness, either practical or theoretical, on depth, and on intrinsic interest. What does not pass at least one of these tests is left behind, "in the literature."

That works of reference are intended to give relatively short and partial accounts of public knowledge means that they cannot, for every purpose, replace the bodies of literature from which they derive. If candidates for inclusion in some representation of public knowledge are not drawn from the earlier literature into reference works but left behind, then that literature must be retained to complete the records of public knowledge. Documentary research will be required to extract them, which is the price we pay for the incompleteness we value in works of reference.

We can take the inventory of existing general and specialized encyclopedias, dictionaries, directories, handbooks, gazetteers, treatises, textbooks, critical reviews, and systematic histories as representing fragments of the complete encyclopedia.[26] There is no satisfactory way of dividing publications into those that are reference books and those that are not. Format will not do as a single distinguishing characteristic: if some "reference books" are in list or tabular format, others are works of continuous exposition. Author's purpose will not do: what one has produced may have values not aimed at. Sources used will not do: a systematic handbook of inorganic chemistry, for example, may be based on massive documentary research, but a telephone book, as good a reference work as any, represents data collected routinely in the conduct of a certain business and is no work of minute scholarship. For our purposes, a work is a reference work to the degree that it can be treated as a section of, or a selection from, an imaginary complete encyclopedia, that is, as a deliberate survey of what is known in some area of inquiry, or as a systematic presentation of all, or all of the most significant, facts in some array of facts. This is a crude explanation, but sufficient for present purposes.

Apart from its intentional incompleteness, the apparatus of works of reference we actually have at any time is anything but a unified, trustworthy, and usable representation of public knowledge at the time. The huge inventory of encyclopedias, textbooks, handbooks, guide books, instructional manuals, treatises, critical reviews, dictionaries, directories, almanacs, and the like, represent the independent efforts of thousands of individuals and groups of individuals widely distributed over space and time. The works are of very unequal value as representations of public knowledge as it was when they were made.[27] Whatever their fidelity of representation of knowledge at the time they were made, they lose their fidelity over time, though at very different rates of speed. Since they are largely made independently of one another, they do not completely cover the departments of knowledge with a consistent pattern of varieties of work: one field may be supplied with a treatise but no introductory textbook, another with an old encyclopedia but no periodical reviews of progress. Where reference works containing material that could be useful exist, they may be constructed on principles that are not in correspondence with the user's interests, so that the material can only be discovered by great effort, if at all. These are imperfections in the organization of representations of public knowledge which can be overcome with different degrees of ease.

The loss of fidelity that summaries of knowledge undergo with the passage of time can be avoided if, instead of publishing one's summary as a document, one maintains it as a file and works continuously to revise it. Behind the printed telephone directory is the continually revised file maintained by the telephone company, which one can query by use of the telephone. The scholar who not only publishes his treatise but maintains files of additions and modifications based on continuing research and review of others' research over the whole field of his treatise is engaged in maintaining an up-to-date representation of his field, which is part of public knowledge if indeed available on demand to others. The institutional counterpart of such a scholar is the information analysis center or specialized information center, whose importance was stressed by the well-known Weinberg report, *Science, Government, and Information*: "We believe that the specialized information center, backed by large central depositories, might well become a dominant means for transfer of technical information.

These centers not only disseminate and retrieve information, they create new information. They must be staffed by scientific interpreters, who themselves contribute to science. They make an information center a technical institute rather than a technical library." The tasks of such centers, as described by the Weinberg group, are clearly those first of the maintenance of a representation of public knowledge in our sense, and incidentally of the production of conventional printed reference works. "A specialized information center makes it its business to know everything that is being published in a special field—such as nuclear spectroscopy or the thermophysical properties of chemical compounds; it collates and reviews the data, and provides its subscribers with regularly issued compilations, critical reviews, specialized bibliographies, and other such tools."[28] But the job of such a center is not finished with the publication of a single reference work or set of reference works; it has a continuing responsibility to maintain a currently accurate representation of knowledge in its field. Increasingly in the future, and to some degree now, its currently maintained files will be available directly from long distance; computers and telecommunications will alter the conditions of availability of public knowledge. It is the combination of a continuing effort of analysis and synthesis, and changes in the conditions of access to the current result of this effort, that can overcome the unavoidable datedness of published works of reference.

It is important to point out that the continuing effort of analysis and synthesis is not inherently limited to branches of physical science and technology. Why should one suppose that what is known about biblical archaeology or the history of Tibetan Buddhism bears any less complex relations to the literature recording investigations into those fields than what is known in a field of chemistry bears to its corresponding literature? Wherever what is known bears a complex relation to what is published, the same opportunity for continuing efforts at maintenance of a comprehensive and faithful representation of public knowledge exists. The need for analysis and synthesis in order to arrive at an accurate picture is the same, though the urgency of need may be different. The possibility of new discoveries by the application of thought and imagination to analysis and synthesis is as real in the one case as in the other. If specialized information centers are not established to look after the interests of the humanities and social sciences, it is not because the intellectual requirements of discovering and reporting what is known are different; rather, it is because individual scholars are expected to act as the custodians and conservators of particular branches of knowledge as one-person information centers. Wherever publicly available data are to be analyzed and synthesized, the same opportunity may exist.

It should also be said that the maintenance of a file or data bank is not what constitutes an information center in the sense presently of concern, and the technical means of file maintenance—using computers or using pencils and slips of paper—have nothing to do with the case.[29] A computer-based file of unevaluated bits of data may be said to constitute a data bank, but it is no information center. Critical analysis and synthesis are the crucial ingredients.

The organization of a set of individuals and agencies, each of them responsible for the maintenance of a faithful representation of the state of public knowledge in some specific area and all of them together covering all the branches of knowledge, would be the organization of what H. G. Wells picturesquely described as the "World Brain," "a double-faced organization, a perpetual digest and conference on the one hand and a system of publication and distribution on the other."[30] (The National Standard Reference Data System in the United States represents a fragment of such an organization.)[31] Wells thought of the organization's tasks as including a systematic program of publication of works of reference, starting with the "Standard Encyclopaedia" and including textbooks, specialized encyclopedias, and dictionaries—in short, the systematic provision of a planned apparatus of works of reference for different needs. But the essential prerequisite of this was its function as a "mental clearing house for the mind, a depot where knowledge and ideas are received, sorted, summarized, digested, clarified and compared," just the functions of the surveyor of knowledge described above.[32] Only when a comprehensive network of agencies collectively engage in the systematic maintenance of a faithful representation of public knowledge will the body of knowledge be fully actualized; until then, it is largely an ideal, only imperfectly portrayed in the available apparatus of reference works.

But to have a comprehensive network of agencies systematically maintaining a faithful representation of public knowledge is only one, though an immensely important one, of the desiderata. Public knowledge is not simply an object for contemplation and admiration; it is for use. One purpose of the making of reference works is to make knowledge usable by making it easily discoverable, but needs and interests are so various that no single scheme of organization of public knowledge can be sufficient.

Let us consider the different ways in which knowledge might be organized into bodies, or corpora. Three types of organization are of particular importance: organization on a topical basis, on a disciplinary basis, and on a functional basis.[33] One might undertake to survey what is known about a topic of interest, the Arctic regions, for instance, or the use of leisure time in industrial societies. One might set about surveying the results of the work of the members of an established discipline or knowledge-producing group, such as physiology or sociology. One might try to collect what is known that would be useful to a person undertaking a certain task—what is known that is functionally related to, for example, the job of mounting an Arctic expedition. The same bit of knowledge might turn up in all three surveys, but its context would differ in each. Some of the things known about the use of leisure time come from the contributions of sociologists, and some of these could concern one conducting an Arctic expedition. But sociologists do not confine themselves to the topic of leisure time, nor would the expedition require all of the knowledge there is of leisure time. The first job, in organizing an adequate representation of public knowledge, is simply to determine what *is* known, but that is only the first job. The second job is that of reorganizing it in such ways that those entering into particular situations can easily locate the usable parts of that body of knowledge. Generations of travelers approaching Florence could count on the Baedeker guidebook to tell them what they needed to know; the general task of the reorganization of knowledge for use is illustrated in its most striking, if oversimplified, way by the Baedeker guide books.[34] The general task is that of making it possible for a person to find an answer to the question: What do I need to know in the situation I am entering?

Maintenance of a current representation of public knowledge must be the work of the groups engaged in discovering new knowledge, but those groups cannot be expected fully to appreciate, much less to provide adequately for, the interests of the potential users of their discoveries. If they are responsible for the initial stage of organization of representations of public knowledge, they cannot be expected or trusted to carry on to the second stage of functional reorganization for use. If we think of the first stage as yielding a complete set of independent chapters of a great encyclopedia, the second stage is far more than the job of furnishing an apparatus of cross-references among the separate chapters. It is only a short step in the right direction to instruct the reader of the chapter on Arctic expeditions to "see also" the section on leisure in the sociology chapter. A further step is that of rewriting that chapter (if necessary) so that it will be intelligible to the nonspecialist, but this too is only a short step. A further step is that of excising irrelevancies and overrefinements (irrelevant and overrefined from the user's point of view), a job very painful to the specialist, for whom the details and refinements are just what causes pride. But excising irrelevancies and overrefinements is at the same time recognizing or creating relevancies and utilities; recognizing relevancies is finding or establishing a connection between a task and a piece of knowledge; and recognizing overrefinement is recognizing the limits of the applicability of knowledge. Selection requires recognition of relevance and prediction of future applicability. This may be easy: a preestablished machinery for application of new information may be at hand. It may also be an act of invention: a new theory, a new technique, or a new way of altering and operating with information may have to be provided. It may then be the discovery of a new piece of knowledge, namely knowledge of a way of connecting knowledge and action. Such discoveries are unlikely without an intense preoccupation with, and understanding of, the tasks for whose performance applicable knowledge is sought. The reorganizer of knowledge aiming to supply the needs of those wanting to use knowledge for practical ends must be oriented in quite a different direction from the surveyors who simply want to determine what, if anything, a field of inquiry has yielded. Functional reorganization is not merely routine manipulation of representations of knowledge. It is at least selection, requiring awareness of relevance and limits of applicability, and it can be discovery of new ways of making use of old knowledge.

The job of reorganization is not done at this stage; the future user must not only be given what can be used but also instructed in its use. When, where, under what constraints, with what degrees of caution, with what reservations, and how knowledge is to be used—the reorganizer must spell these things out lest the knowledge be used blindly or not used at all. This is a strong requirement that often cannot be met; we are certain of relevances and applicability where we can give no precise instructions for use. But nothing is less rewarding or more frustrating to the person of whom action is required than to be given a mass of information claimed to be somehow relevant but no well-developed means of making use of it. Suspected relevance is not a satisfactory basis for functional reorganization of knowledge. Provision of specific guides to use is the right goal, even if it is frequently unattainable.

It is easy to see that the job of reorganization is another inevitably incomplete one. It is a task of reorganizing what is known around the demands of situations requiring action, but one can foretell situational demands only in rough outline. The common needs of a traveler approaching Florence could be anticipated in the Baedeker guidebook: similar people on similar journeys would face similar situations and need similar information. But it is hard to believe that, even for the travelers to Florence, every contingency could have been anticipated. If we tried to imagine a complete reorganization of knowledge, what could it be but one that would anticipate *every* concrete occasion for the use of knowledge? This reorganized encyclopedia would bear the title *Everything One Needs to Know to Meet Every Possible Situation.* To give the title is to exhibit the impossibility of the job. No one can describe in advance the whole range of occasions for the use of knowledge, and no set of descriptions of merely typical situations, with displays of the knowledge useful in those situations, could be adequate to the use of knowledge in situations that are never merely typical.

If we cannot have a complete reorganization of knowledge, we can have as many partial contributions to the job as we like. And the job of reorganization need not be, and is not, the exclusive concern of writers of reference books. It is the explicit concern, for instance, of professional schools.[35] A person entering a profession requiring specialized knowledge expects to be shown what are the things he needs to know in order to become proficient; every preprofessional and professional curriculum is an attempt to answer that question. Deciding what to include in a curriculum is deciding what will be most useful to the future professionals in the situations in which they are likely to find themselves, and this is simply a particular instance of the general task of reorganization of knowledge. Professional groups develop their own autonomous bodies of working knowledge, but the faculties of professional schools are expected, among other things, to engage in a continuous review of the state of knowledge, with the aim of identifying usable findings. But the professional curriculum has the same limitation as does the specially prepared book of instructions—it can only prepare one for typical situations. The professional school and its curriculum are perhaps the principal social agencies for the reorganization of knowledge, but even they are not adequate means for making the best application of existing knowledge in particular situations. Other social agencies exist, and more will doubtless be created, to help achieve the particularity of reorganization that is ideally wanted. The "think tank" that attempts to survey available knowledge in the light of a particular problem situation, the professional consultant, the independent research agency, and the legislative policy analysis group are all social creations to be understood in part as social responses to the need to bring public knowledge to bear as effectively as possible in particular cases.[36]

Only a small part of public knowledge has any discoverable use, however, except as a basis for the pursuit of more knowledge. The occupational specialists in knowledge may pursue knowledge for its own sake, and what they find may indeed be of interest only in itself, not in its applications to action in the world. When we look into the stock of public knowledge for what will help guide our actions, we may find little there of use; a large stock of knowledge may provide little guidance to action.[37] But public knowledge is only part of the knowledge that may be available to us. Public knowledge is our common stock of articulate knowledge, but we know that much knowledge is not public (not having been made public), and we suspect that much could not be made articulate. What is missed in the survey of public knowledge is not only what people will not tell, but what they could not tell, and what they do not know they know. We want to make the best use we can of the articulate knowledge we have, and surveying it and reorganizing it for use are necessary to that goal. But public knowledge will not take us as far as we need to go. Organization of public knowledge is only part of the job of bringing intelligence to bear on the conduct of our lives; another part of that job is the social organization of people who know more than they do or can say. The organization of knowledge is more than the organization of documents and more than the organization of the evaluated and synthesized contents of documents; it is also the organization of knowers.

PRIVATE IGNORANCE

PERSONAL INFORMATION SYSTEMS

No one's internal image or model of the world incorporates more than an imperceptible fragment of the knowledge represented by the sum of encyclopedias and other works of reference in which public knowledge is formulated, and there may be little similarity in content or even in basic structure between a person's internal model and the public representation of the world.[1] Some people have impoverished though reasonably accurate images of the world; others have elaborate and wholly fantastic notions of what there is. But it is not our concern to examine the ways in which people's internal representations of the world differ from one another and from public knowledge. We are concerned now with the sources of change in one's image of the world in adulthood. More narrowly still, we are concerned with sources of change in the images of the world of adults who have passed the period of conventional formal education. By the time adulthood is reached, the general character of one's view of the world is fixed: the basic structure is settled and the details fairly well filled in.[2] The image continues to change throughout life, mostly in relatively minor ways, though sometimes there are sudden major changes of the sort we call conversion. Some of the changes may be thought of as autonomous, taking place without specific external occasion, as a result of inner mental shifts and displacements. But most are due to learning from what we observe and what we hear from others. These are the changes of interest here.

Everyone has some set of habits or routines for keeping his internal model of the world up to date. It is not merely that everyone's model changes over time, but that there are habitual patterns of exposure to just such information as will bring change. Personal observation and communication are the major ingredients of the habitual patterns. We routinely monitor our environment, keeping track of the current state of significant variables: the weather, the supply of food in the refrigerator, the condition of the automobile, and so on. We have friends, relatives, work associates, and acquaintances to whom we talk regularly and with whom we exchange news and views. We have habits of reading and watching and listening to public vehicles of communication—newspapers, television, radio, magazines, and books. These are not random, but patterned activities. The frequencies of these regular activities vary, from the daily inspection of the weather and weekly reading of the news magazine to the annual Christmas visit to distant relatives and the quinquennial medical checkup. They are not all done at regularly spaced intervals; a regular habit need not be a rigid habit. Some, but not all, of them are primarily devoted to acquiring information. Different communications media serve different purposes, and no one need serve a single purpose. We look at television in part to find out what is happening in the world, and in larger part for entertainment, amusement, and stimulation. We talk to work associates to receive and give information, but also for simple companionship and to pass the time. Here we are concerned only with the gathering of information, and it is clear enough that we can and do regularly gather information in the course of activities, some of which are mainly directed at that goal and some of which are mainly directed at other goals. If I regularly visit friends primarily for the pleasure of their company, still they may constitute a regular source of information on some variety of topics.[3] Those activities that are primarily devoted to the acquisition of information are subject to considerations of yield and cost; we may drop one source of information that is not yielding enough and take up another. Information seeking is purposive and adaptive; information is in part acquired because it is deliberately sought. If it fails to be found in satisfactory quantity and quality where it is sought, we are likely to seek elsewhere. It is also found where it is not specifically sought, as an accidental concomitant of routine activities with other purposes or as pure accident. But if it is true that much of what we learn, we learn accidentally, still it is clear that we could describe individual patterns of information-gathering activity, both where the search for information was the primary motive and where it was incidental, that would account for a substantial part of the change in one's detailed view of the world. The sources of information entering into this patterned activity constitute what we will call the *monitor system.*

Since the sources composing the monitor system are of two kinds, personal observation and communication, an inventory of the system would also fall into two parts. Each item in the inventory might (the job can be done in many ways) consist of three elements: a source, a topic, and an indication of the frequency with which the source is consulted on the topic. In the observational component of the inventory, the sources are simply the places where we look; in the communication component, they are the people we talk to and the communications media we use. A single source may appear in the inventory several times in association with different topics and frequencies—a newspaper consulted daily for international news and weekly for society news, a person consulted almost daily on one topic and infrequently on another. Different sources may be consulted on the same topic: we may get our local political news from many different sources. Evidently, a bare listing of source, topic, and frequency would omit much that we would have to know in order to understand why a particular source/topic/frequency combination occurred in a list. Equally evidently, however, there are enough regularities in our behavior to make such an inventory a longish one for most people.

Not all of the sources belonging to a monitor system will be utilized with great frequency. But there is a particular group of sources that may never be utilized at all and yet may constitute an important part of one's information supply—one's potential, rather than actual, supply. The inventory could contain a large number of elements in which the frequency was given as, "in case of need." This inventory could not be constructed from observation of one's behavior, for the occasion of need may not arise, but it could be constructed on the basis of questioning. A particular person or reference work may figure in one's life as an established source of information on a certain topic even though it is rarely consulted, and even if it is never consulted, so long as it is known to be available for consultation at need. To the monitor system we therefore add the *reserve system,* consisting of the sources irregularly or never used but still known to be available for use.[4]

Parallel to the monitor and reserve systems is the *advisory system.*

Everyone has some more or less elaborate plan for obtaining advice from others in the making of decisions.[5] Except for the most bereft and isolated, there are people to whom we can turn in time of need not simply for information but for counsel; they are available for consultation in case of illness, financial difficulties, legal troubles, and a host of less threatening matters, and they can be used as sources of advice on everything from how to keep one's cakes from falling to how to achieve tranquillity of mind. As in the case of sources of information, we could inventory a person's sources of advice in a standard format of source, topic, and frequency. (Personal observation is not clearly part of this system, but divine guidance frequently is.) The same sources may figure in the inventory of advisers and in the inventory of information sources, but the roles are clearly distinguishable. An informant may tell us about the stock market, providing, for example, inside information about likely future behavior of prices, but he might be unable or unwilling to tell us what stock to purchase. An adviser would recommend stocks, and though he might supply an explanation of his recommendation, we might be happy to take the advice without bothering to listen to the story. An adviser is a source of knowledge as well as the informant, but it is a different sort of knowledge. An adviser tries to answer the question: What is the best thing for me to do, in my circumstances? The answers to such questions, when they can be trusted, are worth more than any quantity of mere information. We may well doubt that, in a particular area of choice and action, anyone can advise us; either no one knows more than we do ourselves, or knowledge is not what is needed. Even in such cases, however, we can welcome external sources of recommendation, for they may at least suggest alternatives we have not considered, or supply a useful nudge to our own imagination.

Advisers come in personal and documentary forms; we not only consult people but their writings, in newspapers and books. But personal advisers have for us the immense advantage that we can ask them the question and not simply note their advice on questions they themselves have selected. They can fit advice to the circumstances of the particular case and the particular time, as documentary sources cannot with any exactness. Documentary advice must be more or less impersonal, directed to circumstances of a given type. Whether our own circumstances fit the type is exactly what one needs to know but cannot find out from documentary sources. This is why we should not take legal or medical advice from documents on the basis of an apparent fit between our situation and the typical situations described; unmentioned features that actually are found in our case may make the advice inapplicable and positively harmful.

A personal adviser may play an important further role: instead of simply seeking advice on how we should decide in a given case, we may delegate decision to an adviser.[6] We will not take someone as an adviser unless we think he knows more than we do in the area in which he advises, nor will we take someone as adviser unless we think he has good judgment, that is, is good at applying what he knows to the circumstances of our case. We may take as an adviser someone whose values (preferences) differ greatly from our own if we think we can trust him to adopt our values temporarily while deciding how to advise us, or if we think we can adjust his advice to reflect our own rather than his values. If we are truly convinced that, as to decisions in a certain area, our adviser knows more than we do and is a better judge than we are of what is the right thing to do in our circumstances and in the light of our values, then we may quite reasonably be prepared in advance to act on his recommendation—in effect, to delegate the decision to him. We often do this when we put ourselves in the hands of a doctor. No doubt we are often mistaken about the qualifications of others, and no doubt we may come to grief by delegating decision. But we can also come to grief by failing to delegate decision. I may decide to act against the advice of one who I think has more knowledge and better judgment than I do, remembering the fallibility of all humans and hoping I will turn out to be right in defiance of present appearances. But delegation of decision is still, in many circumstances, the most sensible, as well as the easiest, course of action.

There is nothing surprising in the fact that people figure so largely as sources of information and advice in almost everyone's information-gathering system.[7] If one's sources were chosen on purely technical grounds, personal sources would often be preferred, for people have advantages as information sources that impersonal sources lack. Every medium of communication is better adapted to some purposes than to others. Documentary sources have their technical advantages—portability, availability to private isolated study, and ability to store indefinitely both large quantities of small pieces of information and long presentations of complex arguments and expositions, to mention only the most obvious. They are not good for the visual representation of motion or the audible representation of sound, and they take so long to prepare as to be inferior sources of the most recent information. Worst of all, they are not able to converse.

We can converse with people and (often) get quick answers. We can ask them, in effect, to reorganize what they know to bring it to bear on a problem and to select from their stock of knowledge the things that we should know. We can ask them to use our problems, our interests, and our capacities as bases for the selection, organization, and presentation of part of their stock of knowledge, or as bases for the giving of definite advice. They are supple and adaptive sources of information, as documentary sources are not. Anything a personal informant or adviser might tell us could be part of a documentary record, but documents do not reorganize themselves and rewrite themselves on demand to fit new questions. It is natural, then, that when we have a choice, we should prefer personal to documentary sources and, in particular, that when we want information to be brought to bear on a particular problem, when we know what the problem is but do not know what we should know in order to solve it, we should prefer personal to documentary sources. If we have an adequate supply of personal informants and advisers, we have no need of documentary sources from which to try to discover what informants and advisers can tell us directly.

We have, in the foregoing, used the terms *information* and *knowledge* as if they were interchangeable. Another person is a source of *information,* we draw on another's stock of *knowledge*—we could interchange terms in those expressions without radically changing the sense of the expressions. It is worth dwelling briefly on the distinctions we would find if it served our purpose (as it does not) to look for them. Having knowledge is having a certain sort of ability. Another person cannot give me knowledge; all he can do is tell me what he knows. But telling me what he knows *is* giving me information; information is the content (the semantic content) of the message uttered in telling what one knows. (We have to distinguish content from message if we are to say that different messages can give the same information—for instance, messages that are statements in different languages. We can, alternatively, identify the message with the content, and say that the same message can be given in different words or ways. In that case, "information" and "message" become equivalent.) I may fail to understand, or may misunderstand, the message and so fail to acquire the knowledge it conveys. Or the other person may have been misinformed, or may have lied, in which case we will deny that what was said represented knowledge at all, though it conveyed (misleading or incorrect) information. The term "information" can be used in a neutral or in an evaluative sense:

the neutral sense, in which any intelligible utterance conveys information, whether accurate or inaccurate, or the evaluative sense, in which information is contrasted with misinformation. We never ask others for information except in this evaluative sense. The information one has about a matter is, simply, what one knows about the matter; when we ask for information, we are asking others to give us some of their knowledge in the best way they can, by saying what correctly represents their knowledge. In telling what one knows, information and knowledge are logically distinct; but in other cases the distinction vanishes. If we learn by observing rather than by reading or listening to what people say, there is no message and so no information (the semantic content of a message); we acquire information, to be sure, but this is now the same as acquiring knowledge. This sketchy, oversimplified account of the relationships of knowledge and information (which entirely ignores the technical notions of information that are in use among specialists) may suffice to justify the common practice, to which we shall adhere, of using the terms *information* and *knowledge* as if they were in general interchangeable.

CONCERNS AND INTERESTS

We have so far discussed only the bare abstract skeleton of personal information systems. The particular content of a system, the varieties of information that one will try to obtain, can be understood only by reference to personal concerns and interests.[8] Let us start with concerns.

All of us suppose ourselves to have some control or influence over things that happen in the world. There are things we can do or bring about or prevent solely by our own effort, and there are things we cannot do by ourselves but which we can influence in one direction or another. These spheres of control and influence are surrounded by an immensely larger background of the things that happen over which we have no influence at all. I may influence, but cannot control, the behavior of my children; I can do nothing whatever about the amount of rain that falls. I can decide what to eat for dinner, and I may have some small influence over what some other people eat, but I can do nothing whatever about the nutritional characteristics of a particular sort of food. Our notions of the extent of our control and influence set the limits of our concerns, for our concerns are the ranges of happenings in the world over which we

think we can have some control or influence and which we intend to try
to influence. Concern is readiness to exert influence: readiness to act,
singly or with others, to persuade, to threaten, to speak up, to do something to bring about desired states of affairs or ward off the arrival of un-
desired states of affairs. Where we think we can have no influence whatever,
we have no concern. This is likely to sound wrong at first, since we clearly
can and do worry about many things we think we cannot influence—the
possibility of earthquakes or of a runaway inflation of prices—and our
worries must be among our concerns. But in such cases the event over
which we have no influence threatens to affect us in ways that we *can*
try to influence; we can at least plan what to do if the catastrophe comes,
and it is only because of its potential effect on a situation that we are
prepared to preserve or defend by our actions that the uncontrollable
event causes worry.

Concern is readiness to act, to exert control or influence, and we are
prepared to act only when we care about what happens. Caring is a matter
of degree, as is preparedness to take action. Ordinarily, one is more ready
to act, the more one cares about what happens, and is not ready to take
much action if one cares little about what happens. If we do care what
happens in some area of life and think we can have influence on what
happens in that area, then it requires explanation if we are *not* prepared
to take action. Of course explanations can be provided. We do not have
the time or energy to do all the things we are capable of doing and must
ration our efforts. Or tactical considerations may lead us to refrain from
attempting to exert influence where we think we could. We may withdraw
a previous willingness to take action while continuing to care about what
happens, being no longer willing to fight that fight and leaving the matter
to others. But in that case one is no longer concerned, and it is doubtful
that one really cares. The idea of caring is so closely tied to that of readiness
to act that we begin to think a person does not really care what happens
in an area of life if he is (and thinks himself) capable of exerting influence
and yet refrains from ever doing so. Caring is, in this regard, like believing:
if we do not act as if we believed (that an earthquake is coming, for
instance), it is hard for others to accept our word that we do believe,
and if we do not act as if we cared (about the welfare of the unemployed,
for example), it is hard for others to accept our word that we do care.
Care joined with ability to exert influence ordinarily produces concern,
that is, readiness to take action; concern is engagement, which is something

other than simple preference that things should happen in one way rather than another.[9]

Of course, we can be quite deluded about the extent of our influence. We may have fantasies of omnipotence or suppose ourselves completely helpless when we are not. Both sorts of mistake may be self-fulfilling. The crusader who thinks he can single-handedly change the world may in fact bring about changes that those with more modest self-appraisals could not, and the one convinced of his own powerlessness may contribute to the diminution of his own power. Our own notions of our power, not the reality of the matter, lead us to try, or to refrain from trying, to influence change.

We are all alike in many of our concerns; we all care for our own health and welfare and that of relatives and friends, and we are prepared to take action to ward off dangers and take advantage of opportunities for improvement.[10] We are all concerned with preserving what we find good in our situation in the world and improving those aspects we find unsatisfactory. We are concerned with the ways we get our living, or the ways it is got for us. Many are concerned about careers, life plans involving progressive achievement or ascent of a social or occupational ladder. Most of us are concerned to some degree with public affairs, although the degree of influence we have, or feel we have, is in most cases small, which explains why people often withdraw from participation in public affairs, such as voting. Not all of our concerns are serious; we can be playfully concerned, with the quality of our game of golf or with projects for restoring the reputation of minor authors. Concerns can be wholly unselfish; we are ourselves necessarily the center of our own view of the world, but not necessarily or exclusively the objects of our most serious concerns. Concerns can be wholly intellectual: we may strive, for instance, to improve the state of theory in an academic discipline by taking action in the form of speech or writing.

Overlapping our areas of concern are our areas of interest. I like to keep myself informed about the political situation in Africa even though I think I could have no influence over it at all. I am interested in hearing of major new discoveries in astronomy even though I do not propose to do anything astronomical. A major manifestation of interest in an area is simply wanting to know how things stand in that area, wanting to be informed. Having an interest does not imply caring that things go in one way rather than another and does not imply readiness to engage in any action at all. Neither does it imply a lack of caring or exclude action. I can root for my favorite side in a battle that is far outside my sphere of influence. Action and inaction, caring and lack of care, are equally compatible with interest in being informed.

What starts as an interest may become a concern, and what is for a while a concern may subside to an interest. And we may be simultaneously concerned and interested, preparing to take action in some matters and noting with interest what happens in other matters in the same area. Neither concern nor interest necessarily leads one to seek information. I may be extremely concerned over the fate of my soul in the afterlife, without therefore thinking that there is any information I need to get in the present life beyond what I already have. And interest can show itself simply in receptivity to news of a topic rather than in active attempts to find out about the topic or the establishment of regular sources of information about it. That sort of interest can be called *passive,* and the concern that leads to no further acquisition of information can be called *closed.* If we know only a person's interests and concerns, we cannot predict his information-seeking behavior unless we also know which of them are active rather than passive and open rather than closed. Even with this knowledge, we do not yet know where information will be sought, when, how often, or how intensively. But there is one kind of thing we do know about concerns, though not about interests. Given knowledge of a person's concerns, we have some knowledge of what the person *ought* to know. This has to be explained.

The difference between concerns and interests is not simply a psychological one between preparedness to act on the one hand and a simple liking to know what is happening on the other hand. There are logical or quasi-logical features that distinguish them as well as psychological features. A commitment to action automatically gives a structure to information seeking that is impersonal, though socially based, for what information is relevant to a particular concern is a public, not a private, matter, with public standards of criticism.[11] If I know your concerns, I have a basis for recognizing not merely what you are likely to want to know, but what you ought to know; you may fail to see, or fail to agree on, the relevance of some information, but there is something to fail in. There are mistakes to be made. Let us think, for illustration, simply of the matter of the defense or preservation of some position—preservation of health or defense of the welfare of one's family. Undertaking the defense of a position commits one to watch for threats to that position; it is inconsistent—pragmatically inconsistent, we may say—to set oneself the task of defense of a position while refusing to watch for signs of threat to that position. But one can simply fail to see a developing threat, or fail to interpret correctly what one sees. These are sorts of error, of perception, attention, or judgment as the case may be. One may see threats where none exist, too, but in both cases there are objective grounds for saying that one's perception or judgment was at fault. An engagement to action automatically provides a basis for classification of information into more or less and not at all relevant, and a basis for judgment by others that one has or has not properly sought and properly used information bearing on one's field of action.

By contrast, an interest in an area carries no commitments. If you profess an interest in opera, and it appears that you do not care to hear about a new performance of *The Rake's Progress,* there is nothing to accuse you of. If you are hungry for talk of opera today and bored with it tomorrow, you may be said to be unpredictable but cannot be said to be in error. If I know your interests, I have a basis for recognizing what you are likely to want to know, but not for what you ought to know. I can say that I thought you would want to know about that performance of *The Rake's Progress,* but I can hardly say that you ought to know, unless in the sense that you may suffer some social embarrassment from your ingorance, in which case I am suggesting that the matter is one of concern rather than of interest. You can define the scope of your interest in any way that you please, drop it and change it and take it up again at will. Relevance of information to concerns defines itself, we might say, but each of us must define for himself the scope and character of his interests.

THE SOCIAL ORGANIZATION OF KNOWLEDGE

Dr. Johnson's remark is well known: "Knowledge is of two kinds. We know a subject ourselves, or we know where we can find information on it." He was right so far, but wrong in continuing immediately: "When we enquire into any subject, the first thing we have to do is to know what books have treated of it. This leads us to look at catalogues, and the backs of books in libraries."[12] That is where inquiry would have led him, but not most of us. Not where, but from *whom* we can get information is our first question. And we are not without ideas on where to look.

An important part of our view of the world is our view of what other people know. In part this view is personal and detailed, in part impersonal and generalized. This person, whom we know, is full of knowledge about sports and the stock market, that one is a mine of information about the private lives of opera singers and pre-Socratic philosophy. Beyond our knowledge of what particular other people know, we expect to find differences in knowledge associated with different social and demographic characteristics—education, sex, religion, geographical location, for example. The inhabitants of Astoria, Oregon, know more about Astoria than New Yorkers do, and vice versa. Catholics know some things that Baptists do not, and vice versa. But particularly we expect to find knowledge systematically distributed among occupational groups. The social distribution of knowledge is thought to parallel the social division of labor; what one does for a living determines in large part what one knows. And surely this belief is, on the whole, correct. If we wanted a single clue on the basis of which to guess how much a person knew about the world in general, then education rather than occupation would be the best clue to have, but if we wanted a clue to what, not how much, a person is likely to be knowledgeable about, occupation would be the best clue to have.[13]

Modern industrial societies are firmly based on an elaborate division of labor, and that division is exhibited in a socially defined structure of positions, or jobs, which can be named (job titles) and defined (job descriptions). A job description is a specification of a bundle of tasks to be performed, tools and procedures to be used, knowledge and skill, and physical and mental characteristics required. Of course, there are plenty of unconventional and idiosyncratically defined jobs, and large differences in degrees of standardization of jobs, but there is enough similarity in the way jobs are organized and defined so that classification is not an arbitrary process. Given an inventory of positions, different job features can be selected to define different occupational structures. The familiar features of income and social prestige roughly define one structure based on higher and lower amounts of both, but other features would yield other structures.[14] The amount and variety of knowledge needed in the performance of a job would, for instance, yield a different structure; farmers, blue-collar craftsmen, and foremen probably have a larger amount of diverse job-related knowledge than the retail clerks and salesmen who outrank them in the sociologists' prestige scales.[15] Still a different structure is defined in terms of functional relations among jobs—the different stages in the transformation of raw materials to finished products, different contributions to a joint result, and different roles in complex interacting sets of roles. Full understanding of what a job is would require understanding of its place in several different structures, and we oversimplify by speaking of "the" occupational structure.

But also, full understanding would require essentially that one know what one has to know in order to fill the position successfully—the knowledge required for the job. In fact, none of us knows very much about the whole array of jobs; there are simply too many of them. (The *Dictionary of Occupational Titles* lists over twenty thousand jobs under thirty-five thousand titles, and it is not the fullest listing possible.)[16] One can survive in a society with almost no knowledge of the occupational structure, and the young too frequently enter into the structure with an inadequate understanding of alternatives and the consequences of choice. But whether one has a good or a poor understanding of the occupational structure, one's view of that structure is in large part one's view not only of the kinds of work that are done, but of the kinds of specialized knowledge that exist. And this understanding is important to one's information-seeking behavior, since what one thinks there is to look for sets limits to what one will look for. It is hard to imagine social ignorance so complete as to involve unawareness that there are people who specialize in fixing teeth or selling alcoholic beverages, but any of us may be surprised at any time by discovering new occupations of whose existence we had not known (or which we thought had vanished— fletchers and exorcists, for instance).

To be sure, our understanding of this structure is a critical one; we do not accept every occupational specialty as one able to perform the tasks that define it or as having the knowledge necessary for task performance. Those who accept the fortune tellers as able to do what they say they do might reject the claims of the academic knowledge occupations, and one who thinks that surgeons have a real ability may doubt that psychoanalysts do. Here is the individual basis, as well as the social reflection, of the social establishment of knowledge occupations, which is simply one aspect of the more general phenomenon of social acceptance of an occupational group's claims to be able to perform a certain function.

There is another feature of our understanding of occupational structure that is of importance to information-seeking behavior. People are known by what they do; the most salient characteristic by which we identify each other is occupation. But in a similar fashion, bodies of knowledge are identified by what is done with them; we may say, metaphorically, that bodies of specialized knowledge are known by what they do. Where we cannot associate a named body of knowledge with a set of things it allows one to do, it remains elusive and hard to grasp. Cartography is that body of knowledge—one may have no idea of what exactly is in the body of knowledge—that allows people to produce the maps we are familiar with. Helminthology is—lacking an idea of what helminthologists *do,* one lacks an idea of what helminthology *is.* Our ideas of the specialized bodies of knowledge associated with occupational specialties are, perhaps, mostly ideas of functions and enablements. It is different with our ideas of, say, the geographical distribution of knowledge. If I expect the man from Astoria to know more than others about Astoria, I have a quite clear idea of the sorts of things he would be likely to know, and I could comfortably ask him specific questions about his stock of knowledge. But we may be quite incapable of formulating specific questions about an occupational specialist's knowledge; we may have no idea of what sorts of things he knows. But this is only a conversational disadvantage, for insofar as we understand his occupational functions, we can ask questions and set problems within his sphere that call on him to use that unknown (to us) body of knowledge. Further, occupational position is a prima facie indication that he himself does have, and is able to use, the knowledge associated with the occupation. One of the most interesting things to know about anyone we encounter is what we might ask that it would help us to know; information and advice others have that they are willing to share with us can be, as we very well know, of value to us. Our ability to place a person in the occupational structure, then, both gives us a way of identifying the knowledge he is likely to have (namely, whatever it is that allows one to do what people in that occupation do), and a reason for supposing that his knowledge is real; and we identify his knowledge in terms of things done with it, some of which might be done on our behalf. By contrast, our idea of what a person knows, not identified in functional terms, is apt to be so meager that we do not even know what sorts of questions it might allow him to answer, and if it is not occupational knowledge, we lack an important primary reason for trusting that it really is knowledge. To get access to a body of knowledge not identified with functions it allows one to perform, one must know enough to formulate particular questions about the content, but functionally organized knowledge can be accessible to one who is wholly ignorant of its content, so long as he has some grasp of the functions it enables one to perform.

If our understanding of the occupational structure is an important part of our view of what bodies of specialized knowledge exist, our understanding of the institutional structure of the society provides us with our view of how that specialized knowledge is put to work and of the conditions under which, and to whom, it is available. Knowing the occupational structure is knowing that there are such people as dentists, geologists, television repairmen, and the like; knowing the institutional structure is knowing in what kinds of settings these positions are actually occupied—what kinds of organizations, available to whom, and under what conditions. The institutional knowledge is knowledge of where I could go if I needed the help of those whose occupational specialty gives them knowledge I need to have used on my behalf. But the institutional structure itself also serves as the basis for a further organization of knowledge. The individual working in a particular setting naturally accumulates knowledge of work-related things—about the people with whom one works, about the setting in which the work goes on, and about things affecting the conditions of work (markets, customers, bosses, unions, economic conditions, laws, regulations, informal and even illegal opportunities for avoiding the objectionable features of the work setting, and so on). The size of the job, the amount of independence and responsibility, the amount of personal interaction, and the size and structure of the organization within which the work is done, all heavily influence the amount of knowledge incidentally accumulated in the course of work, as well as the kind and amount of knowledge functionally required for performance. This incidental knowledge is also largely functionally related, if not to the technical performance of the work, then to the slightly different matter of life in the world of work. It is knowledge that tends not to be available except from personal sources. If the specialized knowledge used in work that might as well go on in one setting as in another is sought by preference from personal sources, all the more so is the incidental knowledge of the work setting, which perhaps could not be obtained except from those in the setting. This differential distribution of knowledge also influences our view of what is known and who knows it, and so the pattern of information seeking. I seek out a person working in a certain organization if I want to know of unannounced plans of that organization, or how I can get a job in the organization, or the character of a different organization with which that one has to deal daily. Again, it is not where, but from whom I can get information that is the question, and the beginning of an answer is furnished by my prior knowledge of institutional and occupational structure.

So whether one is inside or outside the world of work, one's view of that world is an important structural determinant of one's view of what knowledge there is and where to find it. For those who do occupy a position in the world of work, of course, work is of further and immense importance to one's information-gathering behavior. One's occupation is among one's central concerns in two senses: one's position in the occupational system is a position one is usually strongly concerned to preserve or improve, and, at least if it is a satisfying position, one will be concerned with the work and with the quality of one's work. The existence of these concerns provides the reason for seeking information bearing on the performance of the work and on the maintenance or improvement of one's position in the world of work, while the position itself provides a supply of sources of such information. Work associates are likely to figure largely in one's personal information system, and the social setting of work is a social location for the regular exchange of information. A position within the social structure of work provides a view on the rest of the structure—other occupations, the bodies of knowledge associated with them, and the incumbents of some of the occupational positions. Learning and staying informed about a job and the conditions of work involves learning about the neighborhood or environment of the job, including further sources of information. The need to make a living provides incentive for information gathering, and the technical character of the work and the social setting provide determinants of what sort of information will be gathered (determine the relevance structure of the information gathering), while the social setting provides a supply of sources for one's monitor, reserve, and advisory systems. Some of these sources may be imposed rather than freely chosen; training, reeducation, and instruction may be supplied without being sought. The character and setting of the work may heavily influence one's information-gathering behavior away from work, as when one is expected to devote time off the job to study for the sake of improvement of one's abilities. Since one's occupation also largely determines the extent of the resources (time, energy, and particularly money), one has to pursue information gathering, and since the occupation one has strongly influences one's own and others' expectations of what else one will or should be concerned with and interested in, it is hardly too strong to say that occupational role is the most important single clue to understanding personal information gathering. Nor should this be surprising, since occupational structure is the key to class and status structures in society as well.[17]

While one's occupation is central, it is not usually one's only link to the institutional structure or the only avenue to specialized knowledge. Labor unions, political organizations, religious organizations, and social, cultural, and philanthropic organizations all may be links to further worlds of specialized knowledge. In a highly organized industrial society with complex division of labor, being cut off from institutions, being outside the occupational structure, and having an imperfect idea of institutional and occupational structure lead as well to being cut off from access to knowledge. None of us has very much knowledge, but most of us have access to a great amount and realize that we have.

Obviously, the occupational structure of a society and its associated distribution of specialized knowledge do not account for the whole social distribution of knowledge. But it is an approximately systematic, and hence knowable and usable, basis of distribution. Particular private concerns and interests may lead to the aggressive pursuit of specialized knowledge outside and independent of that structure. For particular individuals, voluntary activities, social and political involvement, hobbies, and amateur scholarship produce individual "pockets" of specialized knowledge that are often greater and more intensely cultivated than the specialized occupational bodies of knowledge. But this distribution has to be discovered bit by bit, individual by individual, without much guidance from knowledge of social organization. There is, of course, one further systematic basis for the distribution of knowledge that does account for a large part of that distribution, namely, the distribution of private knowledge of personal history. Everyone can be counted on to have more information than anyone else about his own inner and outer life (which does not imply that others cannot often describe us better than we can do ourselves). Counting items of knowledge is not at all straightforward, but it seems reasonable to suppose that most of what anybody knows falls into one of two categories: private knowledge of personal history, and knowledge accumulated in the occupational role. Most of what anyone knows, then, consists of things that most other people do not know.

We spoke in the first chapter of the task of reorganization of knowledge around the needs of particular fields of application, which is a matter of attempting to help what is already known to find its appropriate uses. There is a different, and perhaps more important, sort of reorganization of knowledge whose possibility we must recognize though its treatment is beyond our scope: the reorganization of the occupational structure of society. The structure of the occupational system changes constantly, as do the stock of knowledge available to be put to work and the social requirements or expectations associated with different positions in the occupational system. Jobs disappear, new ones come into being, old ones are reorganized to include new sorts of responsibility, new practices supersede old ones within an occupation, and entrance requirements are revised for good or bad reasons. All of this motion in the occupational structure constantly revises the social distribution of knowledge simply by alteration of the character of the positions in the occupational structure. Structural change in the organization of society's work leads to structural change in the distribution of knowledge. Technological change is a major, but by no means the only, cause of occupational change; the rationalization (and at times the "irrationalization") of work is an independent cause. A deliberate attempt to alter the organization of work could result from political change, aiming at more satisfying arrangements of tasks and more equitable allocation of rewards, an alteration that would both lead to and perhaps depend on a change in the social distribution of knowledge.

But can we imagine a reorganization of work leading to a uniform social distribution of knowledge, that is, leading to the disappearance of specialization in job and job-related knowledge? The social division of labor, on which the social distribution of knowledge is based, can be seen as itself a human disaster; so it was by Marx and Engels, in *The German Ideology:*

> As soon as the distribution of labour comes into being, each man has a particular, exclusive sphere of activity, which is forced upon him and from which he cannot escape. He is a hunter, a fisherman, a shepherd, or a critical critic, and must remain so if he does not want to lose his means of livelihood; while in communist society, where nobody has one exclusive sphere of activity but each can become accomplished in any branch he wishes, society regulates the general production and thus makes it possible for me to do one thing today and another tomorrow, to hunt in the morning, fish in the afternoon, rear cattle in the evening, criticize after dinner, just as I have a mind, without ever becoming hunter, fisherman, shepherd or critic.[18]

But the freedom to turn from one job to another does not abolish the need to learn what is required to do the job (if it is to be done well), and it takes time and effort to learn. The decision to learn some set of jobs, instead of the need to learn just one job, still means not learning some other set of jobs, and so specialization will not disappear. But there is nothing wrong with occupational specialization in knowledge as such. It is stupid jobs that are the problem: the problem is a *poor* division of labor, not the fact of division.

It is clear that questions of the distribution of knowledge in society touch immediately on profound questions of the whole social, political, and economic organization of society. What might seem a relatively superficial distributional phenomenon is actually a reflection of society's deepest realities.

THE LIMITS OF INFORMATION GATHERING

No one pursues information to the exclusion of all other activities; life would soon stop if one did. In the first place, maintenance of an information system is costly; it uses up time, effort, and money. In the second place, there are limits to our ability to understand and use information that could be got if we took the trouble. In the third place, we can have enough—enough useful information to satisfy our wants, and enough interesting information to sate our appetites. Let us review these conditions, with a view to seeing whether we can understand the way we arrive at a particular level of information-gathering activity and the way the level changes over time.

Reading, watching television programs, listening to the radio, and conversations all take time, and an astonishing amount of people's time is spent in these activities. After sleep and work, use of the mass media is the largest single consumer of time; together with social gatherings and conversations outside the work environment, it takes up almost all of the free time left after work-related activities (working and going to and from work) and the satisfaction of basic needs (sleep, eating, and personal care) are counted up. Among adults in industrial societies, work-related activities and basic needs take up more than 80 percent of the total time fund; a little more than four hours a day, on the average, are left as free time, distributed, of course, very differently across the week. Much of this time is devoted to the mass media as a primary activity, much more to the media as a secondary activity (e.g., listening to the radio while eating and reading on the bus to work). Of the approximately four hours of free time, about three are occupied with the mass media, among which television is predominant, the degree of its predominance depending on its availability.[19] (This is an international average, and there are large local variations. Americans have about an hour more free time and spend it on television.) Clearly, this is not time spent in the pursuit of useful information or information relating to interests; most of it is for entertainment, at least in America. The amount of time spent in pursuit of information is modest. "Reading pamphlets, newspapers, magazines and the like may not occur every day, but an overall minimum average of some 15 mintues seems to be quite universal across countries for keeping oneself somewhat informed," and television or radio news programs are perhaps the principal additional media used for information gathering.[20] Clearly, time could be reallocated within the category of free time (more information, less entertainment). But the category of free time is not, after all, a very large one, and information gathering is an activity that has to compete with many others for the limited quantity of free time. People who say that they have no time to read presumably do not mean that work and sleep occupy their whole time; they mean that their time is fully occupied with other activities which they choose not to give up in favor of reading. The limited quantity of time, the limited quantity of free time, and the relative benefits or rewards obtained or expected from spending time at one rather than another activity are all matters of the highest importance in understanding information-gathering behavior.

Not only time, but also effort is expended in the acquisition of information. Physical effort is rarely in question, except in cases like that in which one has to walk a long distance to reach a particular information source. It is intellectual effort, or cognitive strain, that is in question. I may be able to read a foreign language with difficulty, which means that not merely more time is required to read a passage, but more work. Things written in one's native language but employing an unfamiliar conceptual inventory are more work to read than those employing a familiar one. Stylistic features influence readability, but conceptual features are more important barriers to ease, as well as speed, of comprehension. Novel and difficult ideas, as well as complex syntax and hard words, make for work on the part of the reader or listener. And so a source of what would be valuable information may be shunned, simply because it is too much work to extract the information that is offered.

Finally, money is obviously needed for many sorts of information gathering. Personal information sources may be free, but impersonal ones are often expensive. Subscriptions to newspapers, journals, book clubs cost money. Attendance at meetings, conventions, courses of instruction usually cost money. Even the free offerings of television and radio require equipment purchase. Advisers' services are not generally free.[21] Friends and co-workers may advise us, without expectation of reward, but outside the sphere of friends and co-workers, advice usually has its price. Lawyers, doctors, consulting engineers, financial counselors, and even spiritual advisers are in the business of selling their services as advisers. The more highly regarded their services are, the more expensive they are likely to be.

No sharp line divides the sources that are hard work to use from those that are impossible to use because we cannot understand them no matter how hard we work. In most cases, one hopes, it is only the lack of appropriate prior education that limits present understanding. If I had studied chemistry in the past, I would be able to understand writings on chemistry that are now unintelligible. In some cases, the necessary prior education would not have been possible; I could not have mastered the advanced portion of mathematics even if I had tried, and so a large literature is permanently unintelligible to me. I am certain to remain in doubt about which are the things I could never understand and which are those I could understand given sufficient prior time and effort spent in mastering the necessary basic education, because I am not going to make the investment of time and effort required to find out.

What one already knows, then, is an important determinant of what one can understand and thus find out in future; past history limits future history, and those who already know the most are best able to find out more.[22] We can note, further, that what one already knows determines what one thinks there is to be found out and where it might be found. If we are unaware of the very existence of a body of knowledge, we will not look for sources from which we could acquire that knowledge. The limits of our abilities and of the extent to which we have cultivated those abilities are limits on what we are aware of *not* knowing and on our ability to use what we might accidentally find.

The available amounts of time, energy, and money and our ability to comprehend set limits to the kinds and amounts of information we can acquire for ourselves. Even if information sources were all free, the costs of time and energy and the limit of our comprehension would remain; I cannot understand a free chemistry journal any better than a costly one, and it takes as much time to read a free newspaper as one for which I pay. Money can, however, substitute for time and energy, if I can purchase the

services of someone else who will do my learning for me; and if others will
advise and inform me at no cost to myself, then the limits set by my resources and capacities can be overcome. Providing me with free books
and journals that I have neither time nor ability to use is no way of improving my information supply, but providing me with advisers and informants
who do have time and ability is a way of strikingly enlarging my information
supply.[23]

Finally: we can have what we feel to be enough information: enough
to serve as a basis for decision and action in the areas of our concerns and
enough to satisfy our appetites for information bearing on our interests.[24]
If a concern is closed and an interest passive, then we will be satisfied
with the information we already have (our stock of information) and feel
no need for a flow of new information at all. (Remember that what we
have is not only what is stored in our memory, but what is available to us
from our reserve sources of information, and remember that we have advisers as well as informants, the availability of advisers influencing the
amount of information needed in a stock.) If a concern is open and an
interest active, we will want a satisfactory flow of new information. By
the phrase *information supply* we can refer either to a stock or a flow of
information, or to both, as need arises. An information supply can be
relatively satisfactory in the sense that the attempt to maintain a larger
supply seems not worth the cost involved. It can be absolutely satisfactory,
too, in the sense that one thinks that even if there were no costs involved
in pursuit of further information, one's situation would not be in the
slightest degree improved by further information, because one has either
all the information there is or all that one could conceivably use. But
relative satisfaction is more important than absolute satisfaction. Most
of us do not suppose that we know all there is to know relating to our
concerns and interests, and we could reallocate time, energy, and money
to the pursuit of more information. That we stop where we do can be
explained, without recourse to the presumption of absolute satisfactoriness, in terms simply of relative satisfactoriness. I may not be at all satisfied with my knowledge of medicine or finance, or with my current supply
of information on those areas of concern, when I think of all I do not
know that might be useful, but I am relatively satisfied in that I think it
would not be worth the trouble it would take to extend my knowledge
and enlarge my current intake of information. I include in my monitor
system sources that give me what I think is a relatively satisfactory supply

of information in those areas, and though I could include more sources of still more information, I will not do so, for I think that the benefit received would not outweigh the costs in time, effort, or money. If I feel that my information supplies are not relatively satisfactory, I will look for sources whose addition to my information system will bring the supply up to a satisfactory level. I may not be able to find such sources, and I may not be able to afford them if I find them, but I will at any rate be receptive to new sources if they can be had on satisfactory terms. If, on the other hand, I feel that my information supplies are not only relatively satisfactory but more than adequate, I will be ready to thin out the supply in order to reallocate resources of time, energy, and money to other purposes. This may not happen, since there may be no pressure to reallocate. If I feel that some of my sources are not yielding useful information at all or not contributing anything new to my supply, then I will be inclined to drop them, even though there is no pressure of need from other quarters. If my supplies are adequate, all the sources are positive contributors, and I am not under pressure to switch resources to other purposes, then my information system will be in equilibrium, tending neither to increase nor decrease. Waste is avoided by elimination of noncontributors, and marginally useful sources are retained so long as there is no pressure on resources. In this equilibrium, while one is receiving far less information than one could receive and utilizing far fewer sources than might be utilized, one has what one feels is enough information.

KNOWLEDGE AND DECISION

When we are concerned, we are prepared to act, and we inform and instruct ourselves, and seek advice, so that we shall act effectively. If we think we are receiving enough information bearing on our concerns, then we think we have all the information we need in order to notice occasions for action when they arise and to decide what action to take. We have, we think, an adequate basis for decision. If one reflects, it is not at all clear how one could come to such a conclusion; presently we shall try to see how one could have a basis for this important and somewhat surprising conclusion. But it will assist us if we first review what is known about the different ways in which knowledge can enter into a decision. We shall not ask how people do or should make decisions; the theory of decision making, like the theory of belief and judgment (of how we come to believe what we do on the basis of what we see and hear, and of how we make the particular judgments we do) is beyond the scope of this book. What concerns us is simply the variety of ways in which knowledge can make a difference in decision making, both by its presence and by its absence. We shall concentrate on decision (rather than action and planning for action) and pretend that decision always precedes action (though we know that is not so), and that planning precedes decision (equally false), and that we can take the problem of decision as representing the crucial point at which knowledge and action join (not so obviously wrong).

Let us concentrate on decisions that are made after some explicit deliberation, private or public—after some thinking or talking about alternative courses of action, about the pros and cons of the alternatives, about the likely consequences and likely advantages and disadvantages of different courses of action. We do not always make decisions on the basis of explicit prior deliberation, but we do it sometimes, and those occasions provide the clearest illustrations of the point we want to make. Let us simplify matters further by supposing (what is not far from the truth) that we could have a verbatim transcript of the process of deliberation, where everything said, out loud or silently to oneself, is laid out before us in the style of the minutes of a public proceeding. The particular elements of our knowledge that are explicitly represented in this transcript are those that we will say are used in the decision-making process; they are the elements of our knowledge that are explicitly put forth, laid out for public view or appearing on the stage of private consideration. We can classify them in terms of their function in the process of deliberation, or argument. Some of them are part of the recognition of an occasion for action (We must *do* something, because . . . .); some of them are part of the setting forth of alternatives (Here is one plan of action that is worth considering. . . .); some of them are part of the evaluation of the chances of success, and the consequences of the alternatives (If we do that, we are likely to find ourselves faced with this situation: . . . .); and some of them are part of the counting up of the advantages and disadvantages of the alternatives (That result would really be in our long-range interest, because . . . .). These are not independent functions; the upshot may be that the alternative courses of action are all so disagreeable that, after all, it is better to do nothing, so that what enters into the final stage of the deliberation may take one back to the initial stage. We must not suppose that the decision arrived at is in any sense determined by the course of the deliberation; what we explicitly take into account in the deliberation may have no effect on the decision, and the decision may not be a recognizably inevitable or required one given the preceding deliberation. Often enough, decisions, particularly those on frequently recurring matters that become routine, are taken after consideration that goes according to a well-defined pattern, with outcomes predictable from the transcript of the deliberation. But also often enough, decisions are not predictable from the transcript. Still, knowledge represented in a transcript of a deliberation is knowledge used in making the decision that eventuates from the deliberation.

When we recognize a piece of new information as potentially useful, we recognize occasions on which it would be used. This piece of information is useful because it concerns signs of the need for action; it would enter into the first stage of a deliberation. That is useful because it would help predict the outcomes of action; it would enter into the third state. The usefulness of information lies in its guiding of our actions, and the way the guidance works can be seen by imagining possible courses of deliberation. But any piece of information might be useful in some conceivable circumstances. We distinguish between the more and the less likely to be useful and discard the latter as practically useless. Useless information, for any particular individual, is information whose role in deliberation he cannot imagine, or else whose role he can imagine, but in situations he considers unlikely to occur. I would not know what to do with this piece of information, that is, I cannot imagine its fitting into a transcript of a deliberation. I know what could be done with this piece of information but will never have to do it; I expect no occasion to arise on which this sort of deliberation will be needed. We estimate the usefulness of information by imagining uses, and where we cannot imagine a use, as also where we can but think the case will never arise, we judge the information useless. Of course, we can be mistaken—the case will arise that we thought would not arise, and the case we expected to arise may not. So we can underestimate or overestimate utility. But we do estimate utility, we do recognize information as something we can later use, and if we expect to make frequent use of it, or use it in important decisions, or if we expect that the use might be crucial, then its utility is judged to be relatively great. We judge information not only in terms of utility but in terms of comparative utility.[25]

But not all of the knowledge that enters into decision making is used in the sense described; not all appears on stage. The things that occur explicitly in a deliberation and would appear in a transcript are based on, or backed up by, knowledge that we do not make explicit and that we would have great difficulty in making explicit, if we ever could at all. When we try to say why we think this plan of action more realistic than that, why we think this outcome more likely than that, why we trust this person more than that one to carry out a plan effectively, or why we are more confident of success today than yesterday, we can often say no more than that is the way we feel. These are matters, as we say, of judgment, and we do not expect that a person whose judgment we consider to be good will be able to tell us precisely and in detail what makes him offer this judgment rather than that.[26] Nevertheless, we think such judgments to be informed, to be based on accumulated knowledge. We think judgment has a basis in knowledge, even when the judge cannot set forth that basis in detail. And the basis is, at least in part, specific: things noticed in the past make us now trustful or distrustful of this person, and once-learned facts and theories are in part responsible for our suspicion that this plan cannot work or our confidence that it will. The influence of such specific pieces of knowledge may be remote and indirect, and we may be unable to discover the tendrils of influence, but we nevertheless suppose that information enters specifically into informed judgment, even if in undiscoverable ways.

But much of what we know affects our deliberations and decisions in less-focused and nonspecific ways; it colors our deliberations, but diffusely rather than at particular spots. It enters neither explicitly nor specifically into deliberation, but it is the background that influences the ways in which we deliberate and the light in which we see the situations in which we find ourselves. Background knowledge determines point of view. We do not expect people from different cultures to see problems in the same way, nor do we expect people in a single culture but from very different occupational groups or with very different educational backgrounds to see problems in the same way. We justify some sorts of education, not by reference to the applicability of particular items of knowledge to specific sorts of future decisions, but by reference to a diffuse change in the entire way in which decision problems are viewed. The knowledge we acquire works in us but is not explicitly used at all, and particular items of the knowledge are not directly influential on particular judgments or steps in deliberation. (We cannot even be sure that we still have the knowledge that diffusely influences our way of viewing a situation; the process of learning may leave an altered way of approaching problems after the things learned have been forgotten.)

Lack of the knowledge that is displayed in judgment, and lack of the background knowledge that influences the perception and treatment of decision problems, can be as harmful as the lack of useful information that could enter directly and explicitly into deliberation. We all recognize this, in others if not in ourselves, blaming poor judgment on lack of experience (in the course of which the relevant knowledge would accumulate) or blaming narrow and short-sighted views of a problem on lack of a sufficiently broad education. But there is a large element of sheer guesswork in such diagnoses, for we do not have accurate ways of estimating the effects of experience and education on decision. The future utility of particular pieces of information can be seen quite straightforwardly, in many cases, by the easy invention of a context of deliberation, an argument exhibiting clear logical patterns. But the future effect of particular sorts of experience and education can only be guessed at. It seems plausible to suppose that we are prone to large errors of estimate in this regard, vastly over- or underrating the future effects of study and experience. Enthusiastic friends urge us to read books that, they think, will change our whole lives, but both the looking forward to a changed life in consequence of reading a book, and the looking backward to discover particular incidents that changed the character and direction of a life, are speculative adventures of great risk. Hardheaded, pragmatic people argue that only experience can give the knowledge needed for sensible decisions, but if that knowledge, in part at least, never enters explicitly and consciously into deliberation, the hardheaded view must be based on a more or less softheaded guess. The effects of knowledge and experience are largely unconscious, and it is not surprising that we should find it difficult to make accurate estimates of their nature, size, and value.

COSTLY IGNORANCE

We may think we have enough information, but we may be badly mistaken in that view. First, let us try to distinguish harmless from harmful ignorance, and then we will go on to consider how we discover that we suffer from the latter.

Ignorance is sometimes a problem calling for solution, but certainly

not always so. I cannot read Sanskrit or shoe horses or repair space vehicles;
I might prefer to know these things than not know them, but my not
knowing them represents no problem calling for solution. I know nothing
of Malayan history, of the liturgy of the Eastern church, of the classification of the Foraminifera, or of the sources of the early writings of Marx.
I suppose I would rather know about these things than not know, though
I have no strong preference either way. But these areas of ignorance are
hardly areas of troublesome ignorance. The reason is obvious enough:
I can envisage no situation arising in which I am likely to require such
knowledge. I can imagine no situation that is at all likely to arise in which
such knowledge would help me in the least. Others need to know such
things, but I do not. I am none the worse for my ignorance, so far as the
conduct of my life is concerned. If a full and more accurate view of the
world is always preferable to a partial and less accurate view, still we have
to admit that many sorts of ignorance are not practical disadvantages, and
that many improvements in fullness and accuracy of knowledge are not
practical improvements in one's ability to cope with one's situation.

But, of course, much ignorance is of the problematical sort; ignorance
is often disadvantageous, and it is in our own interest to keep the amount
of our own disadvantageous ignorance to tolerable levels. It is costly ignorance that we have to worry about.[27]

It is sometimes easy enough to recognize cases of costly ignorance. We
make a decision on the basis of what information we have. We subsequently
acquire a new item of information on which we comment: Had I known
this when I was making up my mind, I would have decided differently,
and better; I would have avoided making what was in fact a disastrous
mistake. We are sometimes sure that a piece of information would have
been crucial in the sense that without it, a decision went one way, but
with it, the decision would have gone another way. When the outcome
of the more informed decision would have been better from our point
of view than the outcome of the less informed decision, a loss has been
incurred. Sometimes this can be put in straightforward terms of money:
if I had known what I now know, I would have done so and so, and saved
so many dollars. Often it cannot: we say we would have been better off
deciding differently, but can give no answer to the question "How much
better off?" in terms of money or any other unit of value. Such crucial
bits of information, lack of which results in decisions whose outcomes
are less desirable than would have been the outcomes of decisions made

in view of the lacking information, furnish the best and clearest cases of costly ignorance. That there are such cases cannot be doubted, and their avoidance is clearly a desirable goal.

Costly misinformation is a special case of costly ignorance; if the wrong decision is made in the light of misinformation, and correct information would have led to a better decision, then the correct information was crucial. Costly advice can be viewed similarly: the wrong advice is analogous to misinformation, leading to the wrong decision.

It has to be recognized that, as there is such a thing as costly ignorance, so there is costly knowledge. For it also happens that we regret decisions taken on the basis of knowledge and wish we had not known what we knew. I wish you had not told me what you did about so and so, we say, for it led me to vote against him and for his opponent, who subsequently turned out to be a worse scoundrel than any. Information can be inopportune; coming when it does, it leads to decisions we regret. We may think that all such cases are really cases of costly ignorance, that it is only because the inopportune information is partial that it leads us to decisions we regret, and that in the light of fuller information the consequences would have been such as we would have desired. But it is not clear that there is any sense at all to be made of the notion of "full" information, nor have we any right to certainty that the more information we have, the better our decisions. We can, as we say of others, misuse knowledge, and we can be simply unable to make any use of knowledge. Whether we use it or not, that is, whether it occurs in our conscious deliberation, it may have an effect on us, and the effect of a bit of knowledge may be as harmful as the effect of the lack of a bit of knowledge.

What we have said of costly ignorance gives us a clue to understanding information needs.[28] Writers on the topic of information needs have had some difficulty disentangling wants and wishes and demands from needs, and understandably so, for the term *need* is a complicated one full of implicit reference to goals to be attained and to the notion of good and ill as well. But we can offer an explanation of need that may be generally if not invariably useful. Crucial information, lack of which would result in a worse decision, is needed information; information that is lacking but has no such effect is not needed. The lack of crucial information causes harm, in the form of worse decisions than would be taken in its presence; the lack of noncrucial information does no harm. And what could one be said to need more than that, the lack of which causes harm?

By parallel argument, of course, costly knowledge is knowledge that causes harm, and hence is knowledge whose absence is needed; in this case it is ignorance that is needed. In both cases what is needed is what brings about a better decision, in the sense of being a cause of a decision; this is a causal, not a logical, sense of *need.* In both cases, the effect could come about without our awareness of having or lacking the information in question; need is independent of use. Clearly we can need what we do not want, and want what we do not need; in our terms, this is simply the fact that we can be unaware of costly ignorance and mistaken about what sort of ignorance would be costly. Need is relative to a goal to be attained, namely, making better decisions; this seems to capture accurately the ordinary sense of the term *need,* which is always need for something. Since what seems better to the agent may seem worse to the external observer, disagreements about need can arise that reflect differences in the evaluation of outcomes achieved. In this respect, our explanation of need is consistent with common sense and usage, since disputes about needs reflecting differences in standards of evaluation are a regular feature of common use of the term. If we accept this account of needs in terms of costly ignorance and costly knowledge, we will at least know what we are talking about, though we have not provided any easy way of recognizing particular needs.

We can define a "logical" sense of information need too, in terms of a pattern or model of correct (or proper, or optimal, or rational) decision making. We can put it in terms of our notion of the transcript of a deliberation: information is logically needed if, without it, a transcript cannot have a particular decision as its correct result or conclusion. (The transcript is thus like a formal argument, which cannot have a certain decision as conclusion without certain information as premise.) Where we do not specify the patterns that transcripts must take, where decisions are not definite functions of transcripts, and where one is concerned with success in attaining desired results rather than the correctness of decisions, the logical sense of need is inapplicable.

We have so far spoken of costly ignorance only in connection with decisions taken as a result of deliberation, but there are other sorts of decision to be accounted for. First, decisions are often taken without explicit deliberation, without any conscious period of reflection and calculation at all. This does not or need not imply that they are poor or stupid decisions, that intelligence is not used in making them, or that they are

made without information. It simply means that there is no conscious
setting out of alternatives, calculation of consequences, or evaluation of
the likelihood and value of different outcomes. We can still say, retrospec-
tively: had I known what I now know, my decision would have been
different and better. Our willingness to say this simply confirms what we
have argued already, that information affects decision without being consciously used at all, that is, without our being aware that, and how, particular pieces of information work in leading us where we go. We ourselves
engage in "psychohistory," the reconstruction of an unconscious biography.
When we say what we would have done under different circumstances or
when we make hypothetical backward predictions, we are speculating
about ourselves as much as any external observer. The notion of costly
ignorance applies to decisions taken without conscious deliberation as
much as to those taken on the basis of deliberation; no changes are required for application of the notion to such cases.

Costly ignorance can be involved also, however, in the host of cases
in which we do what we do without anything that could be identified
as the making of a decision at all. This is most obviously the case when
we act on the basis of habit. I do not engage in anything that could be
called decision at all when I eat my breakfast. Sometimes I do: I consider
whether I want this or that food today, how something is to be cooked,
or whether I shall read the rest of the newspaper or a journal article while
eating. But these are exceptions. I could deliberate about any of the
things I do that I have in my power to do differently; the range of actions
I take is part of the range of my field of choice. But I do not deliberate
about most of my actions, and if I tried to do so, action would cease.
Costly ignorance, if understood only in relation to decisions, whether or
not accompanied by deliberation, would be too narrowly understood;
it must be seen in relation to our habitual behavior and indeed all our
behavior that could become the subject of choice, whether it ever does
so or not.

The extension is easy enough, but it suggests how convoluted are the
workings of information in influencing action. One pattern of behavior
may be more advantageous than another, as one particular decision may
be more advantageous than another, since a pattern's advantage depends
on the advantages of particular instances of the pattern. Receipt of new
information can lead to reevaluation of patterns of action and a decision
to change one's ways, or it can result in a change of ways without any

conscious reevaluation and decision. In the former case, the analogy to costly ignorance in single decisions is almost complete: not knowing the crucial fact, we continue our practice; but receipt of the crucial information would have produced reevaluation and change. This is analogous to the case of crucial ignorance of occasions for action: not knowing the crucial fact, we do nothing, but receipt of the crucial fact would have produced recognition of an occasion for action. But then we extend the notion to cover cases where new information would produce change without deliberation and conscious decision; in ignorance of the crucial fact, we continue a practice which would have changed had the crucial information been received. Costly ignorance is that, then, in the absence of which we make worse decisions and continue worse patterns of action. It is, of course, not required by anything we have said that information received should work instantaneously or over any particular period of time at all; costly ignorance can be quickly repaired only if crucial information works at once, but we have no way of knowing in advance how fast crucial information received will work, if at all. For costly ignorance may be irreparable; even presenting the crucial information in the most palatable possible form may lead to no change of behavior.

Indeed, we may suppose that much costly ignorance is irreparable. For ignorance may consist in lack of a large quantity of experience or education, not simply in the lack of a single small item of information. Whether a piece of information can have any effect on us will depend on the whole history and present texture of our mental life; so, paradoxically, information I lack that would be costly if lacking in others may not be costly to me, since I lack so much else on which its effect would depend that it by itself could have no effect on my decisions. It is the background lack that is costly; it is the experience and education that I lack that are responsible for my poor decisions; and it may be simply too late to repair those deficiencies, even if I could (given the lacunae themselves) come to recognize them and to be persuaded that they were costly. That we can understand what costly ignorance is, and recognize instances, does not mean that we can always repair it.

Nor does it mean that we can measure it and say how much the cost of ignorance has been for someone during some period of time. To do so, we would have to be able to compare the outcomes of decisions actually made with outcomes of the decisions that would have been made, given a different (and better) history of changes in the state of one's knowledge.

We think we can do this in some particular cases, though our confidence is that of hindsight; much of the knowledge we now have, especially about the outcomes of decisions, we could not have had at the time of decision. (The comparison body of knowledge cannot be a state of omniscience; how do we know what choices an omniscient being would make? That leaves us great latitude in specifying the comparison histories of knowledge states, by reference to which "ignorance" is to be specified; but the only practically interesting sort of costly ignorance is ignorance of what we could have known at the time of decision but did not.) If we can do this in some cases, we plainly cannot do it for a whole life or a whole time segment of a life. Nor can we do the next required thing, namely, calculate in numerical terms the values of the outcomes of actual and hypothetical decisions in order to compute the cost of ignorance by comparing the values of outcomes actually obtained with the values of outcomes that would have been obtained in consequence of decisions that would have been taken in a better state of knowledge. The project of measuring costly ignorance during a life or part of a life is hopeless.

It follows from this, incidentally, that we cannot measure the value of changes in our information-gathering practices. The value of a change of practice (a change in information flow) could in theory be measured by comparing the cost of ignorance when decisions are taken on the basis of one information supply with the cost of ignorance when they are taken on the basis of an altered supply. The difference in these two cost figures would be the value, positive or negative, of the change; positive if the cost of ignorance goes down, negative if it goes up. We could not measure the value of the change simply by comparing the values of outcomes of decisions made under the two information-supply conditions, for then we would not know whether differences in information supply were responsible for differences in these outcomes. We would change our information-gathering habits to reduce costly ignorance, and we would need to know that the change had indeed done that. But there is an additional complication, in measuring the value of such a change, beyond the already insuperable difficulties of measuring costly ignorance. Measurement of the value of changes in information systems would require knowing how our states of knowledge would change, consequent on specified changes in information-gathering arrangements. We would have to say how change in information flow would change our beliefs, as well as how these changes would be reflected in decisions. But we cannot, in general, say in advance (or in hypothetical reconstruction of the past) how much of what appears in documents, or how much of what one is told by informants and advisers, will be attended to, believed, or remembered. Not being able to say this, we cannot construct the comparison history of changes in the state of one's knowledge that is required for calculation of costly ignorance.

There are circumstances in which decisions are made on the basis of explicitly formulated patterns, where all the information that enters into decisions enters explicitly, being used in fully specified ways, and where the values of outcomes can be precisely measured. In those circumstances, the cost of ignorance and the value of changes in information-gathering arrangements may be precisely determined.[29] But these are not the circumstances of our ordinary lives or of the most important decisions in any context. In the informal, inexplicit decision making that fills our lives, while we surely suffer from costly ignorance, we cannot say how much we suffer. But we do not need to know how much we suffer in order to be sure that we do suffer and to take steps to reduce the suffering.

HOW MUCH IS ENOUGH?

How do I tell that I have enough information? What signals that it is time to add new sources of information, and what tells us that the addition of sources has gone far enough? What causes us to start, and what to stop, a change in our habits of information gathering?

The final test of the adequacy of decisions is in the consequences. If we are happy, or at least satisfied, with the results of our decisions, we have no cause to complain about the antecedents of those decisions, including the information supply on which they were based. If events turn out well, in our eyes, then we have no basis for criticism of our role in bringing about the events or of the information supply we used. But there are at least two qualifications to this account of the test of success. First, we may think that the happy outcomes of our decisions were matters of good luck, and that bad decisions had good outcomes thanks to events beyond our control. And in such a case, we may not take good results as conclusive evidence of adequacy of decisions or of the antecedents, including information supply, of those decisions. Second, the decisions with happy outcomes may have been taken in acutely uncomfortable ignorance, and we may find the price of discomfort too high to tolerate. But with these exceptions, it appears that we can generally conclude, from satisfaction with the outcomes of decision, that information supplies on which decisions were taken were themselves also adequate. It is the outcomes in which we are interested, not the means whereby the outcomes are reached, and if we get the results we want, we have reason to be satisfied with the means employed. This is simple-minded enough but seems correct just the same.

We can put this differently. We judge our performance in terms of the outcomes of our decisions and actions, factoring out our contribution to those outcomes. If the outcome is satisfactory, we usually credit ourselves with good performance. If it is unsatisfactory, we may still credit ourselves with good performance if we can find the poor outcome due to circumstances beyond our control—other people's failures, natural disasters, and so on. If our own performance is judged satisfactory, we need not worry about our information supply, for it is maintained only to serve the purpose of adequate decisions. Satisfactory performance—coping and maintaining mastery of the ranges of affairs of concern to us—does not lead to change of information-gathering behavior; it is our evidence that that behavior itself is adequate.

It is obvious that evaluations may differ when made from different perspectives. Although I am happy with the results of my decisions, an observer may be most unhappy. Consequently, although I find no fault with my information supply, the observer may find it wholly inadequate. The observer may be in a position to influence my behavior (we shall presently discuss that circumstance) or to make me dissatisfied with the outcomes of my actions, but otherwise, the observer's unhappiness is of no concern to me.

But our decisions do not always or generally lead to outcomes with which we are satisfied. And, in new or changed situations, what has hitherto been adequate may not be still adequate. Let us start with the reflection on past decisions. If such reflection is to lead to change of information-gathering behavior, it must single out the information supply, rather than other factors of the decision-making process and the external determinants of the outcomes of action, as responsible for the unsatisfactory outcomes. We do not blame our information supply for the defeat of a candidate for whom we voted, since the outcome we were trying to influence was one in which our share was very small. We do blame our information supply for failing to give us in time information that, we now think, would have led us to choose another candidate. We blame our information supply for unnoticed opportunities and unnoticed signs of danger. In these cases, there is information we now have that we think we could and should have had earlier; what we now know, we should have known then, at the occasion for decision. Note that this is not simply useful information whose earlier lack we deplore; it is crucial information. Note also that the recognition of the prior lack has two elements: we recognize the relevance of a piece of information, and we speculate that it would have moved us in a certain way had we had it earlier. Both are necessary. We do not blame our information supply for failing to yield irrelevant information even if we think it would have made a crucial difference, and we do not blame it for failing to supply relevant information if we think it would have made no difference. It is clear enough that historical reflection on our decisions is a highly fallible source of information about the adequacy of our own information supply. We may easily fail to realize that decisions with unhappy outcomes were due to information deficiencies, and we may easily go wrong in our historical reconstructions of the decisions we would have taken had our information supplies been other than they were. Nevertheless, such reflection on the past is one of the very few ways we have of determining the adequacy of our information supplies.

Detection of past costly ignorance is one way of discovering the need to revise one's information supply or take some other adaptive step (what others, we shall see). But that requires that we now have information that we lacked in the past (if it was information that was lacking), and it is a matter of chance that we come to have the information and notice that earlier ignorance was costly. There is another way in which we can come to discover what our regular arrangements for information supply have failed to give us, namely, by specific search for information outside our usual channels. Since the point of our usual arrangements for obtaining information and advice is to give us what we need for decision, we will only engage in such a special outside search when we think our regular supply has failed us—when we suspect that we have not got all the information we need. But what leads us to this suspicion is only the existence of an unacceptable decision situation. This is a notion which must now be explained.

When we face a decision, our situation may be unacceptable in any or all of these ways: first, we may be unable to foresee with any certainty the consequences of the alternative courses of action that we are considering; second, we may be unable to decide on the relative desirability of the outcomes that we think likely or possible; third, we may find all of the alternatives unacceptable. Uncertainty about outcomes of alternatives is the topic that receives most attention from students of decision making, and it is both important and ubiquitous. But there are plenty of cases in which we are quite certain what will happen if we take this rather than that alternative, while we are often uncertain about which is preferable among the alternative outcomes we can envision. The world presents us with plenty of decisions among alternatives, all of which are unpalatable and even the least objectionable of which is still intolerable.

An acceptable decision situation, by contrast, is one of this sort: we are able to foresee the consequences of alternatives with a subjectively tolerable degree of uncertainty; we are sufficiently clear about our preferences among the alternatives; and at least one of the projected outcomes is itself acceptable.[30] This triple reference to subjective judgment is unavoidable. One person can tolerate more uncertainty about the future than another, one demands less clarity about what is preferable to what, and outcomes that are acceptable to one are intolerable to another. So a decision situation acceptable to one may be wholly unacceptable to another. A decision situation can, of course, present several acceptable alternatives, and alternatives much more than barely acceptable. But these cases do not concern us. If a barely acceptable decision situation does not lead one to conduct a special search for information, a fortiori the still better situations will not.

We assume that, faced with an unacceptable decision situation, one first makes use of all one's usual sources of information. One tries to remember whatever one has already learned that would help one improve the situation, consults one's reserve supplies of information and regular advisers. If no improvement comes about, there are many things one can do besides search for more information. We may do nothing and put off decision in the hope that with the passage of time, the situation will change—more information will arrive automatically through our usual channels, new alternatives will occur to us, or chance will turn up information or alternatives. We may pass on the decision to another——delegate it, pass the buck, put it into wiser hands. We may withdraw from the situation entirely—get out, leave town. We may accept the unsatisfactory situation—lower our hopes and expectations to match the perceived situation, thus turning the unsatisfactory into a satisfactory situation. (This is a strategy recommended by the ancients.) We may try to change the nature of the decision problem—enlarge, or narrow, or redefine the situation and change the character of the decision to be taken. Or we may try to change the external situation itself—take action against a sea of troubles, make inventions, undertake political action, start or join a revolution—in short, act indirectly to change the initial situation in which the decision was faced. These are all different ways of avoiding an unsatisfactory decision by altering or getting out of the decision situation. And we use them, as appropriate, often enough.

Or we may continue to confront the decision situation as it is and seek to improve our own ability to cope with it. If time is available, we may seek education, formal or informal, at the hands of teachers or by means of textbooks or other educational materials.[31] Or we can seek experience: put ourselves into situations in which we will improve our ability, for example, to judge the likely consequences of actions. We can set ourselves to make observations, conduct experiments, test alternative courses of action on a trial basis. Or, finally, we can seek useful information from new informants or new documentary sources. We can, of course, try a combination of these. Whether to do one or more of these things is itself a decision problem.[32] It is the sort of problem we may solve in a purely habitual way, always seeking to escape, always procrastinating, or always going to the library. Or we may solve it by explicit deliberation. If the decision is to search for new informants or new documentary sources of information, and if the search is successful in that it yields information that transforms an unacceptable into an acceptable decision situation, then we have prima facie evidence that our regular information-gathering behavior has not been adequate, for if it had been adequate, we would not have had to resort to the special search.[33] It is not the existence of unsatisfactory decision situations that constitutes evidence of inadequacy in our information system, for the fault may lie in the limitations of knowledge in general, not merely our knowledge, or it may lie in the nature of the world, which insists on presenting us with inescapable and intolerable choices. Rather, the unsatisfactory decision situation is the stimulus to search for help, and if we find it in outside sources of information, that is the evidence that our prior arrangements have been inadequate.

Finally, of course, we may accept the unsatisfactory decision situation as it is and simply make a decision. One can always make decisions on any given amount of information, and the decision may be the right one. It is true that some people may be unable to make decisions no matter how much information they possess, and anyone may suffer temporarily from a complete paralysis of the will. In a psychological sense, no amount of information, however large, may be large enough. But in a logical sense, no amount is too small. There is nothing impossible, in principle, about making a decision on no information, since one can always toss a coin and decide to decide on the basis of whether heads or tails comes up. Seeking information is itself costly, and one has no assurance in advance that the search will be fruitful. So one may decide to decide on the basis of what information one has, and the results may be no worse than they would have been if a search had been undertaken.

ADAPTATION

We may find, in one of the above ways, that our regular information-gathering arrangements have failed to give us some crucial information or that our advisers were advising us in the wrong direction. It is then time to consider a change in information-gathering habits or in the roster of advisers. Whether we change and what changes we make will depend on at least the following factors: the sources of information and advice we discover to be available; our ability to use the available sources of information; what we are prepared to spend in time, effort, and money; how productive of useful information or trustworthy advice we estimate the sources to be; and the seriousness of the failures of the prior information system.[34] These are all interdependent factors. If the failures of the prior system seem serious, we will be prepared to make a relatively large investment in new sources. If they are too serious, we may withdraw from action in an area of concern entirely rather than secure new supplies of information. If they are not at all serious, we may make no change unless it can be done easily and without significant cost. Other things being equal (as they never are), we will prefer more productive rather than less productive sources of the sort of information we should have been receiving but were not receiving, and we will prefer the less costly (in time, energy, and money) to more costly sources. We will look for a new combination of sources (which might be all of the old sources plus one additional new source) that will, at the least cost, bring our information and advisory systems up to a level of adequacy, that is, to the point at which we are relatively satisfied with our supply of information as a basis for decision. Here is our hypothesis about people's information-gathering behavior: when they discover costly ignorance due to failures of their information system, then, provided it is neither too small to worry about nor too large to be remediable, they alter the composition of their monitor, reserve, and advisory systems in the least costly way that will yield what is again a relatively satisfactory information supply.

(This may strike one as an overly rationalistic or overly calculating picture. But we are not saying that people consciously engage in calculation; all we are claiming is that this description fits their actions. We can achieve a result without consciously aiming at it. As to the question whether this is a picture of rational behavior, many would say that it was not, since it portrays people as tending to provide themselves with what they feel to be only relatively satisfactory supplies of information rather than with supplies that include all relevant information. This does not conform to everyone's ideal of rational behavior.)

The sorts of changes made in following this rule may be very small indeed: consulting one's daily newspaper for a sort of information hitherto ignored, for example, or looking regularly at the condition of one's bank balance instead of waiting for overdrawn notices from the bank. For the elements in one's monitor system are numerous, mostly small items, and the adaptiveness of one's information-seeking behavior shows itself as much in tiny modifications as in major reconstructions. But there are occasions for major change, as we shall see.

If we are right in supposing that changes in the information system are made with the aim of finding the combination of sources that will, at the least cost, bring information supplies up to adequacy, then we can go on to infer a number of patterns of preferences that will be exhibited in our selection of new sources, on the basis of the foregoing discussion.

(1) We will prefer to rely on advisers rather than to accumulate education that will enable us to comprehend, and experience that would enable us to apply, information in the adviser's field of competence; this preference will be greater, the less we begin by knowing in the area of his competence and the less frequently we have need of his advice. For the less we know to start with, the greater must be the preliminary investment in education, and the less often we need the advice, the less productive such investment will be. Gaining education and experience is costly in time and effort, and reliance on even a less than highly expert adviser is preferable to such an investment. In addition, the more important the

area of concern, the more investment is required if we are to be our own advisers, therefore the greater the cost.

(2) We will prefer sources that adapt to our needs over sources to which we must adapt ourselves, for it is quicker and easier to get information from the former.

(3) We will prefer sources of specialized knowledge, organized in such a way as to correspond to our areas of concern, over sources not so organized. With respect to personal sources, this means a preference for people recognizably involved in areas of action corresponding to our concerns. With respect to documentary sources, it means a preference for those with a functional rather than topical or disciplinary organization. Those who share our concern are likely to be more ready to understand our information requirements and respond helpfully, and documents organized on functional lines in correspondence with our areas of concern are easier to use. Orientation to decision and action, in both personal and impersonal sources, is preferred over orientation to theoretical, systematic, and taxonomic goals.

These are by no means the only inferences that can be drawn, but they are particularly important for our future discussion. But one assumption made earlier needs review in the light of present discussion. We assumed that the decision to make a special search for information outside one's usual channels was made only with the stimulus of an unacceptable decision situation, so the special search was not only exceptional but also, if successful, a sign of failure of the regular information supply. But it is not inevitable that the special search be treated so. We can imagine a person who has a positive preference for not accumulating information in advance of need, for not maintaining regular information-gathering habits, for avoiding informants and advisers alike, and for solving each problem as it arises by a new search for information. This picture is possible, but plainly not usual. The reasons are apparent. If a single source can serve repeated uses, it is wasteful of time and effort to go in search of another source on each occasion of use rather than rely on the source already known to be useful. If one encounters sources of apparent potential usefulness, it is a waste of time and effort, at least, not to remember the source and mark it as one of the reserves to be consulted at need, and instead to start again afresh as if one had never encountered a source of the information needed. Habits of action, in this as in other areas of life, are ways of saving effort and time. Even if what one seeks can be found as a result of a special search, the search requires thought and time that one would prefer to have free for other uses. A general principle of economy of effort governs the reasonable person's instrumental activities; what we do not for its own sake but for the sake of some further goal, we generally try to do without waste of resources. To make an economical use of our time and energy, as well as money, in the service of further goals is a rule that was neither invented by an economist nor imposed by any discipline of operations research or systems analysis; it is simply the rule of the ordinarily reasonable person trying to make sensible use of his resources. It is the homely virtue of prudence.

In the preceding discussion of decision making, we have been dealing primarily with the use of information in the areas of one's concern. Information-gathering behavior in areas of interest, rather than concern, requires different treatment. Such behavior is adaptive, too, but there is no test of adequacy of supply comparable to the test of costly ignorance. We gather information in areas of interest for no further purpose, so we cannot gauge the adequacy of the supply by reference to the purposes served. There is, of course, a theoretical limit to the accumulation of interesting information, namely, when one has got all there is in the field of interest, but it is not a limit we are likely to approach. What we learn in pursuit of an interest may turn out to be highly useful in an area of our concern, but that is an incidental benefit, not the purpose of the pursuit. We may gather information in part simply in order to have something to talk about with friends or simply to appear well informed to others, the aim being not to use the information or simply to have and enjoy having it, but to display it. Information gathering solely for display seems to be a third sort of activity not assimilable to the pattern of concerns and interests; perhaps it is rarely found in a pure form.[35] Since information gathered to satisfy interest is gathered for its own sake, many of the characteristics we have ascribed to the gathering of information for use may not apply, such as the preference for advisers over development of one's own stock of knowledge, the preference for functionally organized sources, the preference for personal over documentary sources, and the preference for regular, established sources over ad hoc special search. We can even hypothesize that the search for information would take on a derived intrinsic value lacking to the search for useful information; one may enjoy the search for what one would enjoy finding and having. As there are no costs attached to not getting a piece of interesting information, so there may be no concern with the costs of hunting for interesting information, and the hunt may be as rewarding as the discovery. In short, we cannot expect the gathering of interesting information to resemble the gathering of useful information in many of the most significant respects. The two activities, though not completely unconnected, can follow very different patterns, the goals being different and the ways of determining that goals have been reached being radically different.

Perception of failure of one's information system is not the only occasion for adaptation. We modify our behavior in anticipation of changed circumstances and in response to inner and outer changes that change the character of the decisions and actions required of us and so, indirectly, the character of our information needs. If we attain a state of relative satisfaction with our information supply, and thus an equilibrium position, a huge variety of changes can still destroy the equilibrium.

(a) *Changes of position within the environment.* Nothing can so disrupt the pattern of information gathering as moving from one place to another, which brings a new set of personal relations, new informants and new advisers, and different publication media. Change of occupational role is almost as disruptive. Entrance into the work force, retirement from it, change of occupation, and promotion (or demotion) within an occupational hierarchy or on an occupational ladder—all such changes may lead to changes in information-gathering habits due to the informational requirements of new positions or the relaxation of old informational requirements.[36] Temporary changes in level of activity of information gathering about the time of the change may not last, but changes in the content of the information system reflecting changes in specific concerns and interests may be permanent, or last until the next major change. Changes of social position and of role, other than occupational role, bring changes in information-gathering behavior. Interests and concerns partly are cause and partly are consequence of changes in social role and position, and position and role carry expectations on the part of others about what we will be informed of, expectations we incline to fulfill. Barbers are expected to know about baseball, and social climbers to know about the fashionable world; both groups generally do what they are expected to do. Some of us deliberately or obstinately defy expectations, but most do not.

(b) *Changes in the environment.* During times of political, economic, and social crisis, the general consumption of news from radio, television, and newspapers soars, as is hardly surprising.[37] Troubled times mean times in which almost everyone expects changes in the environment to occur at an unusually rapid rate and to be of a sort that may profoundly affect personal concerns; temporarily, the rate of information gathering would be expected to rise. When less is happening, or less that is threatening, the world is offering less occasion for concern, and less frequent and careful scrutiny of change is needed. Changes in the rate of change of the environment may make an old system of information gathering subjectively inadequate—one no longer feels able to keep up. Too great a volume of change might lead to less rather than more information gathering—why bother to try to keep informed, when things change every day?

(c) *Changes in the available sources.* Insofar as people constitute the most important elements of one's information system, their removal from us is as disruptive as our removal from them. People withdraw from our circle, move away, die. Documentary sources change: they cease publication, lose their reliability, increase their subscription rates. With changes in the sources, we should consider changes in our evaluation of the sources. We may come to think that a source is and has been a source of misinformation rather than information and poor rather than good advice, in which case we revise our estimate of its usefulness.

(d) *Independent changes in interest and concern.* Independently of changes in our roles and social location, our interests and concerns shift over time—we get bored, lose interest, acquire new enthusiasms. We withdraw from areas of concern while retaining interest in the same areas; we enter into activities where we had once been interested observers. So the information requirements change.

(e) *Changes in available resources.* As other changes occur in our lives, we find ourselves with more or less time, more or less energy, or more or less money available for information gathering. These changes may themselves suffice to produce changes in the information system. We have, at some stage in life, more money than time, and so prefer less time-consuming information sources that may be more expensive in money; at another stage, we have more time than money, so prefer less expensive but more time-consuming sources. A decline in energy may lead to a general decline of information gathering as well as a decline in level of concern.

(f) *External requirements on performance.* We may be satisfied with our own information supply and with the decisions we make, but others may be dissatisfied and in a position to encourage or force a change in our information-gathering behavior. Those for whom we work or those controlling the conditions under which we are allowed to practice a profession may impose their own standards of adequacy on us, and the threat of loss of job or of license to practice may be highly effective in changing our information-gathering habits.[38]

All of these sorts of outer and inner change disturb the equilibrium of the information system and provide occasions for its modification. We may not react, for the disequilibrium may not be uncomfortable. But over time, our habits do tend to change in response to such outer and inner changes; information-gathering behavior adapts to changed circumstances.

THE LIMITATIONS OF
PERSONAL INFORMATION SYSTEMS

Our attempt at a synoptic picture of personal information-gathering systems has been a sketch of a vast and complex range of phenomena of interest to a bewildering variety of different specialists. We have deliberately ignored most aspects of the use of mass media that are explored in communications research; we have not discussed, for example, the myriad motives for such use or the range of gratifications derived therefrom. We have not tried to describe the ways in which people come to accept or reject, believe or disbelieve, the messages that come to them, or the ways in which those messages get transformed and the ways they transform the individual's view of the world. We have not tried to say what patterns are found in the explicit use to which information is put or in judgments based on unarticulated stocks of information; nor have we tried to say whether decisions are often in conformity with normative, rational models of how decisions ought to be made.[39] Investigations of all these topics can be expected to illumine our inexact and tentative picture.

More immediately to the point, we have said nothing about the level of activity or of amount of information actually acquired through information systems; we have tried only to say what determines the level, whatever it is. But we know in any case that the differences among individual information systems are immense, that both the range of concerns and interests and the amount of information intake that is found satisfactory differ enormously from person to person. Empirical investigation, or simple review of what we already know, would reveal many cases of few concerns, narrow interests, and slight information intake, as it would reveal many of extensive concerns, wide interests, and voluminous information intake. Further, we

know that review or investigation would reveal large differences in the
inventories of sources in monitor, advisory, and reserve systems among
people of comparable concerns and interests and comparable appetites
for information. Such differences among preferred sources of information—
for instance, relative dependence on documentary sources as against personal sources, on local as against "cosmopolitan" sources, and on co-
workers as against people with different occupational or social relations
to oneself—would define the individual information-gathering style, style
being best understood in terms of the pattern of one's choices in an area
of activity.[40] All of these characteristics of information gathering deserve
more study than they have so far received. But they are not our present
concern, which is rather the basic features of information-gathering systems,
whatever their extent, level, and style. Let us summarize the main points
argued above about such systems:

They are purposive: they are maintained to collect what we recognize
as useful and what we regard as interesting information.

They are adaptive: they change in level of activity and in direction in
response to changing internal and external conditions.

They are habitual: they reflect a preference for regular continuing
sources of information over reliance on accidental acquisition or ad hoc
search in hitherto unfamiliar sources.

They are economical: they are maintained at a level affordable in terms
of time, energy, and money, and changes are made in consideration of the
productivity and the cost of alternatives.

The components of such systems that collect information bearing on
concerns have these additional features:

They are functionally oriented: they collect information on the basis
of its utility in decision making, and they reflect a preference for sources
that can respond to inquiries put in terms of task or problems to be solved.

They rely heavily on personal advisers: they secure the use of information others have, in the form of advice rather than information, to supple-
ment the individual information supply.

They aim at relative satisfaction: they do not aim at completeness of
information or the greatest possible amount of information, but at the
smallest amount on which satisfactory decisions can be taken. This does
not mean that one tries to avoid having more than the smallest adequate
amount, but that one does not try to have a larger amount.

It is the last feature that is likely to be seen as shocking if true. That we should seek just enough information rather than as much as we can get may seem foolish, if not immoral. But "just enough" is the same as "as much as is needed." If we fail to get information or get misinformation that leads to unsatisfactory decisions, then we have failed to get what we needed and suffer from costly ignorance. This is what we aim to avoid.

If it seems foolish or even immoral to behave in such a way, the reason may be the lingering belief that decisions always get better as the quantity of information on which they are based increases.[41] But that belief cannot be sustained. We have already discussed costly knowledge, which is enough to show that more information can lead to worse decisions. Even if large increases in knowledge lead to large increases in the quality of decision (a point on which there is no certainty), there is no reason at all to think that small increments of knowledge regularly produce small or large increases in the quality of decision. The slightly more learned are not always slightly wiser, and it is no law of nature that the much more learned are much wiser.

The proper concern for personal information systems is not that they aim at less than complete information, but rather that they are likely to fail in attempting to avoid costly ignorance. The proper concern is with our limited ability to recognize the defects of our own information systems. Some of our concerns are, and stay, closed; we simply fail to consider the possibility that our supply of information in a particular area is inadequate. When we do suspect a need for new sources, our search for sources is limited by our understanding, which may be and frequently is imperfect, of what sorts of sources there are—our understanding of what there is to know and who knows it, our understanding of the social distribution of knowledge.

The sources we find may badly misinform us. In most cases, we can recognize that we are being misinformed only by comparing one of our sources with another—a good reason for having a system containing redundancies, but comparison does not show which source, if any, is giving good information. We are not aware of the information that never reaches us at all. We discover by accident the imperfections of our information supply—or we never discover them at all. We have no accurate way of determining the causes of past unsatisfactory decisions. We may fail to

realize that costly ignorance was at fault, or we may blame the defects
of our information system for what was actually due to lack of education,
experience, or mismanagement of the information we had.

We have no accurate way of gauging the utility of information acquired
by education or experience, insofar as that information is not explicitly
used in making decisions but rather enters unconsciously into decision
making. When we choose new sources for our information system, we do
so by sampling and estimating the future usefulness of the information
they furnish, but our samples may not be representative and our estimates
may be poor. Worst of all, nothing guarantees that the information we seek
and find will correspond even approximately to public knowledge, to
what our society knows about the world. If we start with a bizarre or alien
view of the world, we may seek only sources that will be consistent with
that view, and we may well manage to find them and ignore all others.[42]
If our information-seeking activities form a self-regulating system, it is
one that may be and stay radically inconsistent with the view of the world
that constitutes public knowledge. This is, to be sure, a fault only to the
outsider, for inside one's own idiosyncratic world view, it will be public
knowledge that represents error. What looks to the outsider like costly
ignorance or costly misinformation may, to the presumed victim and his
like-minded friends, look like self-evident truth; information about his
errors may be rejected as from the devil. Detection of others' costly ignorance always involves a presumption that one has oneself got the truth
or at least the better view of the world; another's well-meant help may
be rejected as presumptuous. Information systems adapt to changing circumstances, but we cannot trust that they will adapt very well. We may
easily either underestimate or overestimate our own success in providing
ourselves with adequate information supplies. So there is plenty of work
for those whose concern it is to help people get, not all the information
there is, or all that could possibly be useful, but that information whose
absence is costly. It is to the question of the part that can be played by
the library system in this collective effort that we now turn.

THE USES OF LIBRARIES

Those who never use libraries may still want to have large, well-stocked libraries available to themselves and to others. They might suppose that they benefit from the use other people make of libraries, and they might think it important to themselves that libraries be available in case of need, while hoping that the need will not arise. I benefit from the education that others gain, and I benefit from the availability of hospitals that I hope not to have to use. So I can understandably encourage the education of others and the maintenance of hospitals, even though I do not propose to undertake more formal education myself, and even though I hope not to have to sample the hospital's services. If we think of libraries as providing services that benefit only those who use the services, we forget the "spillover" benefits to others that may arise from one person's use of the library.[1] If we think of libraries as providing only what is sought for its immediate enjoyment, we forget that there are services we like to have available but do not like to have occasion to use.[2] If the whole value of libraries accrued to those who used them, then, since a relatively small proportion of the adult population makes much use of libraries, we might conclude that libraries were of no concern to most of the adult population.[3] But the conclusion would be wrong, for the nonuser benefits simply from the availability in case of need of a library even when the case of need does not arise, and the nonuser benefits indirectly from the use others make. How one should calculate the extent of such option values and spillover benefits is a nice problem for the welfare economist; that there are such values and benefits we may ourselves conclude from simple reflection.

Whatever the indirect benefits accruing to the individual by others' use of libraries, it is clear from what we have said above that the maintenance of individual information-gathering systems is in part interpretable as an attempt to avoid having to accrue some sorts of direct benefit, namely, those that come through ad hoc search. In the light of the theory or model of individual information-gathering behavior given above, it is clear that the most satisfactory situation for the individual exists when he has no occasion to search for information outside his regular and established channels. The most satisfactory situation exists, in the areas of concern, when early education has provided an adequate knowledge basis for future use and when regular current sources of information modify that knowledge basis to provide a relatively satisfactory basis for decision, counting reserve supplies and the advisory system into the picture. An analogous picture can be drawn for the pattern of interests. When such a satisfactory situation exists, there are no occasions for search for new sources of information or advice outside one's established pattern of information and advisory sources. The need for a search for new sources to solve a particular problem is a sign of failure of one's information system. Far from welcoming occasions for search, one wants no such occasions at all. If available library resources are small, one may actively seek to increase them, but one may also seek to improve one's personal information system so as to eliminate occasions for search in library collections. Ardent supporters of library service can, with perfect consistency, be ardent avoiders of search in libraries.

This does not mean that one will want to avoid the use of libraries. Not all use involves search. The point must be clarified and stressed. Those who approach libraries may want documents of which they already have specific descriptions, such as authors' names or titles.[4] Or they may want documents of a certain sort, or documents giving a certain kind of information, but have no particular documents in mind. It is only the latter group who are engaged in what we will call *search*. The former know what in particular they want; the latter do not. The former are not looking for a source; they have a source. They are simply looking for a copy of the source. The latter are looking for a source: that is what we are calling *search*.

To a great extent, communal libraries, that is, libraries serving a community, such as the inhabitants of a city, or the staff and students of a school, or the workers in a professional establishment or a commercial or industrial firm, serve simply as places in which to consult, or from which to borrow, copies of documents with which one is already acquainted. There we consult large works of reference that are known to us and are part of our regular reserve supplies of information, but are too expensive or too large for addition to our private libraries. There we consult periodical publications that constitute part of our regular supply of information, to which we could subscribe but do not because of their cost or marginal utility to us. There we obtain copies of books of which we learn through our regular information channels, which we could otherwise purchase through book stores or order from publishers or borrow from friends or co-workers. If the library is preferred over other sources from which the same documents might be obtained, it is because it is quicker or easier or cheaper, or requires less investment in storage space as well as money, to let the communal library provide the documents. Those who are large users of documents, as are many academic and professional people, may have use for more documents than each could afford to purchase for private use, and have marginal need for documents that would not be used at all unless communally provided. The same is true, in varying degrees, for those who are not extensive users of documents. The reference works they are familiar with and will consult occasionally, if communally provided, would not be consulted at all if not communally provided. We are speaking now, it should be remembered, of documents of which the individual has prior specific knowledge—specific known sources of information. Insofar as the communal library houses copies of information sources that figure in one's reserve supplies of information, to be consulted in case of need, the library provides a benefit that is independent of the actual frequency with which the sources are consulted. One's known reserves are an important part of one's "potential" knowledge of the world, representing in part one's preparedness to meet and cope with novel problems. Also, communal provision of documents will be more important, the larger the extent of the reserves one wants to maintain. The same is true of communal supply of publications that are part of one's inventory of periodically consulted sources: it is the more important, the larger that inventory is. If I need to look regularly at two dozen journals and three abstracting services in order to maintain a satisfactory information intake, the communal library is vastly more important than it is if I can do with one or two journals to which I can easily subscribe.

So even if my information system is functioning so satisfactorily that there are no occasions for search, I may make extensive use of libraries, and even when I do not have to use them, I may benefit from their housing my reserve supplies, available in case of need. But providing copies of already known documentary sources of information does nothing whatever to repair unknown faults in one's information system. The point can be made more emphatic by imagining what is not far from an attainable goal: delivery of documents, on demand, by libraries to the user without the user's having to set foot in the library. If, on the basis of a telephone call, I can have a specified document delivered to my doorstep, then the library's function as a document delivery service is clear, but so is the fact that a simple delivery service can do nothing to improve the requests I make of the service. What of all the documents about which I know nothing whatever? What of the store of knowledge represented by the huge fraction of the collection of which I am ignorant? How do its existence and availability improve my information situation? Whether or not one does search for new sources, a library of any size contains sources that might be more useful than any of those that figure in one's information system. Those who are content with their information supply may suffer from costly ignorance, and the remedy may be available on a library shelf. Those who are discontented with their information supply may not think of the library as a place to seek new and better sources of information, but the new and better sources may be there. It is not hard to believe that much that is to be found in libraries would make a significant difference to many who suffer from costly ignorance, and that the unknown contents of libraries are of potential utility to many who in fact go without what the library has to offer. Yet it is, or will soon become, clear that there are major limitations on the improvement in the utilization of knowledge possible through the provision of libraries and library services. These limitations we must now explore.

We are concerned here only with adult information-seeking behavior and its relation to libraries and library services. We leave aside library services to children. We leave aside adult use of libraries for purposes other than the search for information. And we leave aside all search for information except useful information, information of value in relation to an individual's concerns and the decision problems that arise in areas of concern. This is, to be sure, a drastic limitation. But the question of the library's role in the effective use of information as a guide to decision and action is the most important question to ask about library roles. There is an inescapable order of priority of importance on the various categories of library use. It is of less social importance to provide a source of recreational reading than to provide sources of information, and it is of less social importance to provide information sought simply for its intrinsic interest than to provide information sought for its utility. I may privately think that my amusement is more important than your utility, but it is hard to see how a society could decide that everyone's amusement was more important than anyone's utility. It is useful information that must come first in our consideration.

ACCESS TO THE COMPLETE LIBRARY

Librarians are apt to think that the larger the collection of documents available to a person or community, the better is the person's or community's situation in respect to the availability of knowledge. People with meager libraries are worse off than those with extensive libraries; the larger the information supply one has, the better one's situation is, and extensive libraries represent extensive information supplies. There must be some sense in which this is so, but what sense?

Let us try to arrive at an answer by supposing that each of us could have immediate access to a complete library, a library containing a copy of every published record that exists. The technical means by which this library is at our disposal are unimportant; one can imagine any futuristic technology one likes. By whatever means one prefers to imagine, I can instantly have a copy of any existing document. (This is universal physical access to documents.) I am also provided, under any technical conditions one cares to imagine, with all the existing indexes, bibliographies, and abstracting journals as well as a conventional library subject catalog on the model, say, of that of the Library of Congress. Here we limit ourselves, for we are not allowing ourselves to imagine presently nonexistent but conceivable means of bibliographical access to the complete library. I can have any document I want, but I must discover what I want by using the actually existing bibliographical apparatus. Further, we will suppose for

the present that we have no human help in using the library or its bibliographical access instruments; we must do everything ourselves.

For the sake of concreteness, let us specify a decision problem with
which we might confront the complete library. I am trying to decide, let
us say, whether to sell my automobile and rely on public transportation
exclusively, a realistic and, for many, an actual problem. Let us suppose
that the decision situation is unsatisfactory to me in the sense that I do
not like the alternatives, I am by no means sure about the consequences
of choice, and I am not settled in my own mind on the value and importance I ought to attribute to different features of the situation. For instance,
reliance on public transportation puts me at the mercy of others, and I
cannot predict how inconvenient this is likely to become. Are transport
strikes likely to become frequent? Will costs rise sharply? Will service
improve or deteriorate? If I retain my own automobile, will costs of fuel
and insurance increase intolerably? Perhaps I am considering too restricted
a set of alternatives; should I be thinking about moving closer to my place
of work? How much importance should I attach to the time saved by
driving rather than being driven?

Problems like this represent the middle range of private decision problems—not matters of life and death, but also not trivial. They are of medium
complexity as well as of medium importance—not simple problems that
require considering only one or two pieces of fact, but also not insoluble
problems of unmanageable complexity. We must suppose that I have gone
as far as I can toward finding an acceptable solution on the basis of what
I already know, what my regular advisers can tell me, and what I can find
in my known reserve sources of information. Now I have the possibility
of drawing on the complete library for additional help.

All the documents in the library are immediately available to me, but
they are not all accessible to me. First, most of the documents in that
library are in languages that I do not understand and so are linguistically
inaccessible to me. Unless someone else will translate them, they are of
no use to me at all. Second, of the documents written in languages I understand, a good part is conceptually inaccessible to me; I cannot understand
them, though I can understand the language in which they are written.
This includes, in my case, most of the literatures of the physical and
biological sciences, most of the technological literatures, and the more
mathematical parts of the social science literature. Other literatures I can
only imperfectly understand, like the literature of the law. Third, of the

bodies of literature that I can understand, or at least think I understand, only a few are critically accessible to me, that is, in only a few fields do I feel competent to analyze and evaluate the contents of the literature. I cannot by my own efforts decide what is *known* by examination of what is *said* in the literature; I cannot myself tell what is accurate and trustworthy from what is inaccurate and untrustworthy. I am not capable of doing what we described earlier as documentary research in any but a few areas. Confronted with a mass of literature, I cannot trust myself to construct a representation of public knowledge or evaluate works of reference that offer such representations. I do not, to put it briefly, know what to think.

So, while I have available to me a complete library, most of the contents of the library are inaccessible to me in one or more of these senses: linguistically, conceptually, and critically. Most of the complete library is, as far as I am concerned, simply in the way; its presence does me no good, for I cannot understand or appreciate it. Of the remainder, the fraction that is accessible in one of these senses, most will be irrelevant to my problem. I may be able to understand and evaluate a portion of the literature of the history of Scotland, but that literature does not bear on the question whether I should cease to maintain a private automobile. And of the accessible literature that is somehow relevant, much is not usable—I cannot see how to bring it to bear on my decision problem. Supposing that I can understand and evaluate the literature on the history of public transport, I still may be unable to fit it into the context of a deliberation on my problem. So even if the contents of the complete library are accessible and relevant, they may still be unusable. I may recognize that they bear somehow on my problem, but be unable to fit them into the context of any argument.

There must remain some fraction that is accessible, relevant, and usable. But now the question is, how am I to find it? The answer depends on the basis of organization of the bibliographic access tools—the catalogs, indexes, bibliographies, abstract journals. What I would like to be able to do is to present a single question, namely, what is known that I should know in order to improve my decision situation? But the bibliographical access tools will not accept such a question. They are organized on topical or disciplinary bases; they group documents primarily on the basis of rough similarity of content. But documents of roughly similar content may be very different in utility to me, and documents of comparable utility to me may be of dissimilar content. I want documents that bear on my problem. The access tools guide me to clumps of documents of similar content but dissimilar utility, and I may fail to discover more than a fraction of those of utility to me.

Here is a further dimension of accessibility: bibliographical accessibility. A library may contain documents that would be of great utility to me which I do not know how to find, in this sense: starting with a general description of what it is that I want, I lack a way of converting that description into a listing of particular documents. I can have a copy of any document in the library that I want; all I have to do is request it by name or number. The bibliographical access tools are meant to be devices allowing me to convert my initial description, which is not the name or number of a document, into a description of particular documents. But they may fail to give me a way of doing this in particular cases, and I may not know how to use them in any case. The documents I am unable to identify are bibliographically inaccessible to me; they are as good as not there at all. What I do not know how to find is as little accessible to me as what I do not know how to understand or evaluate or use when I find it.

Making documents bibliographically accessible is not simply a job of listing and labeling. That a document which could be of use to me has been listed in a catalog or bibliography under some label or labels (index terms or classification slots) does not mean that I would in fact be able to discover that document by using the catalog or bibliography. Listing and labeling are the bibliographer's ways of helping me discover what I am looking for, but in any particular case the help may be insufficient. What I cannot find is not bibliographically accessible to me, even though correctly (by the bibliographer's standards) listed and labeled, and even though accessible to others who can do what I cannot. If I am to be able to find what I am looking for, I must be able to calculate or guess how the bibliographer would label documents of the sort I want. I must recognize, or establish, a correspondence between my way of describing what I am looking for and the bibliographer's way of labeling. This may be easy. The bibliographer may apply labels in just the same way in which I would. It may also be extremely difficult. The very basis on which the bibliographer lists and labels may be incongruous with the ways in which I describe what I am looking for. There may be a simple way of translating my descriptions into the bibliographer's labels or, on the other hand, substitution rather than translation may be required—not a different way of saying the same thing (as in translation), but the saying of an entirely different thing.

And, in fact, the topical or disciplinary basis of organization of most bibliographical works requires of me that I substitute, for the functional description with which I start, topical descriptions which have been used to categorize documents. But there is no recipe for doing this job of substitution. One can learn to do it more or less well by instruction and practice, which increases the accessibility of documents, but things relatively easily accessible to the instructed and practiced user may be as good as inaccessible to the uninstructed and unpracticed. Even for the practiced user, much useful material may be relatively inaccessible. Expert use of existing bibliographical works does not invariably uncover everything of utility, while it does uncover much of no utility whatever. But few people are experts at the use of existing bibliographical works.

If I am provided with a complete library, then, I am provided with a collection of documents, most of which are incomprehensible, unevaluatable, irrelevant, useless, or bibliographically inaccessible, and hence of no benefit to me directly at all. The portions of the collection that are accessible in all senses and both relevant and usable have to be found and converted into usable inputs to my decision problem by a process that is, in varying degrees, time- and effort-consuming. The usable documents must first be found—the bibliographical search phase of the process. They must then be read, analyzed, compared, and evaluated—the documentary research phase. They must then be applied to the decision problem—the application phase. These three phases may be of different degrees of difficulty. I may find, for instance, that the job of bibliographical identification of useful material has already been done for me, but analysis, evaluation, and application may remain to be done and may be arduous jobs. I may avoid the second phase of the process simply because I do not recognize that it is needed. I cannot avoid the time and effort of reading and trying to understand, but I may not even question the validity of what I read. I might naïvely suppose that whatever is contained in the document collection represents what is known. I might not be so naïve, but might find that what the documents said was all consistent and so proceed as if there were no problems of evaluation. The range of degrees of difficulty and cost in time and effort include, at one extreme, the case in which one immediately finds a single text that one accepts as valid and that tells one just what one needs to know, and, at the other extreme, the lengthy literature search producing a huge mass of documents whose analysis, evaluation, and application is the work of months or years.

Evidently, the maximum extent of the benefit to be derived (whether or not I can derive it) depends on what there is to be found and used in the complete library. In the realistic example we are using, it is clear enough that I simply would not find answers to the particular questions I can think of asking (which may, of course, not be the right questions). Much of what I would like to know is simply unknown, though my own inability to evaluate much of what I find may conceal this fact from me. Much of what I would like to know may be what is private, not public, knowledge; someone could tell me, or at any rate give me good guesses, but no one has published them. Much may be what is not yet published; the complete library cannot supply information in advance of its publication. Of course, I do not know in advance how much is known (though that is not everyone's situation—that is just the sort of thing the expert or specialist does know), how much of what is known is public knowledge, and how much of what is in the process of being made public has reached publication, but I have to decide whether to undertake the job of search on the basis of my own guesses about what I am likely to find, and what I am likely not to find.

This rehearsal of the varieties of inaccessibility can be of help in two ways: first, in understanding the considerations that would explain a decision to undertake a search and a decision not to do so, and second, in suggesting directions of change in library service that would influence decisions and increase the likelihood that such decisions would be positive. Let us begin with the first point.

Almost always, a decision to search for information by unaided use of a complete library would be a decision with numerous alternatives. Some of these were enumerated above in chapter two, and a truly exhaustive inventory would surely be much larger. Search can almost always be avoided; there are plausible, if not completely satisfactory, alternative ways of trying to improve an unsatisfactory decision situation. It would be unrealistic to suppose that full-scale deliberations among alternatives are frequent occurrences, but we can see easily how such deliberations, if they did occur, could sensibly lead to decisions not to undertake a library search. If one thinks it unlikely that there is any information to be found by search, then (unless one is desperate) the decision is likely to be against undertaking the job. If one thinks it unlikely that search will uncover critical, decisive information, the decision is likely to be negative; why go to the trouble of finding what will not change one's situation significantly? If one thinks that, while there may exist information that would be decisive, one is not likely to be able to find it by oneself or recognize its decisive character, again a negative decision is likely; why look for what one is unlikely to be able to find or to recognize when found? If one thinks that there may be information one could find that would require analysis, evaluation, and application of which one is incapable, again a negative decision would be likely (unless, for instance, one could give the material to a friend who could do the job). One or another of these conditions must very frequently obtain, so that while decisions not to undertake search may not be based on explicit deliberation, the material is at hand that would indeed explain a negative decision in terms of what a deliberation would or could make explicit. Any individual must decide in terms of his own expectations in these regards, and, of course, the expectations may be grossly in error. A person with only a sketchy idea of what is known and what knowledge is available in libraries may seriously underestimate the likelihood of the existence of potentially useful documents, and a person unused to libraries may grossly overestimate the difficulty of using them. But we must not suppose that it is only ignorance and unfamiliarity with libraries that would lead to decisions not to conduct searches in them, for the experienced and sophisticated library user may decide against search simply because experience and learning leads to an accurate estimate of the personal costs of the job and the small likelihood of commensurate rewards. It cannot be true that experience with large document collections invariably produces a favorable disposition toward further experience. On the contrary, by giving one an accurate idea of what is likely to be easy and what is likely to be difficult, what is likely to be rewarding and what is not, one's enthusiasm for use of libraries as opposed to other ways of repairing unsatisfactory decision situations may be diminished. Even if one is certain that a library contains useful information, one may correctly decide against trying to discover it.

On various grounds, then, both for the unsophisticated and the sophisticated, a decision against special search for information in a complete library could often be expected.[5] But there is a further matter to consider, which would, in effect, prevent the question whether or not to conduct a search from ever arising for a large number of people. For many people, search is simply ruled out in advance as a plausible alternative. For at best,

a search would yield a document requiring to be read and understood,
and for a troublesomely large part of the population, reading is either not
an available source of information or not a preferred source of information.
But there are many other people who might decide in favor of a search
only if they could hope to find, without too much trouble, a single source
of significantly useful information, while they would decide against search
if they thought they would find no single source but rather a collection of
sources—five, ten, or twenty—from which they would have to extract the
information they sought by a process of comparison and evaluation. Others,
a relatively small number of others, would be prepared to search even in
the expectation that a large number of documents would have to be utilized
together.[6] Let us give a name to the readiness to use documentary sources
of information and calibrate it in terms of the number of sources one is
prepared to use together in relation to a single decision problem. Let us
call it *studiousness.* A person is studious to the degree to which he is
prepared to devote time and energy to the study of new documentary
sources of information bearing on a particular decision problem or an area
of concern, the locus of a cluster of related decision problems. A person is
studious to the degree to which he is prepared to engage in the work of
learning—in the cases that interest us, the work of learning, from documents,
what one hopes will improve one's decision situation. One can learn from
other sources than documents, but it is the readiness to study documents
that interests us. Those unwilling to study at all are studious in the degree
zero. Those prepared to study a single source, but no more, are studious
in the first degree. Those willing to use together any number of documents
are studious, as we say, in the *n*th degree. The first two groups, those of
studiousness of degrees zero and one, are of most interest now, especially
the second of these two. It is not at all daring to suggest that studiousness
is distributed among the population in a most uneven way. A small number
of people are highly studious, a large number are studious in the first
degree, and a large number in the degree zero. A large number of people
are disinclined to engage in any study of new documentary sources at all
in order to change their decision situation; for them, the notion of seeking
a textbook or general introductory exposition of a subject does not represent a live possibility at all. Nor is it daring to suggest that there is a significant difference between the readiness to seek and use a single coherent
package of information, and the readiness to seek and use together more
than a single package. If we use two sources together and both tell us the

same thing, the second source has added nothing except, perhaps, a degree of confirmation. If the two tell us different things, however, the work of using them is greater than the work of reading and understanding the two, for the additional job of comparison, reconciliation, and decision of which to believe is added. Using two sources, in that case, is more than twice the work of using one source, while if the sources give the same information, using two sources is a more costly way of getting what could be got from a single source.

What sets a good communal library off from other sources of documentary material (e.g., book stores) is its provision not merely of simple summaries for shallow interests, but of a complex array of sources from which the individual can piece together for himself what may never yet have been explicitly summarized. The pride of a large collection is its extensive subcollections of the raw materials for documentary research. But, if we are right, it is precisely the opportunity for documentary research that almost no one is willing to consider taking; the ability is lacking, and when it is not, the will is lacking. If one expects that, to learn what might help one's situation, one will have, after a more or less tedious search, to piece together the information one thinks one needs, then, for all but a very few people, the decision will be against search and in favor of an easier available alternative. And there always are easier available alternatives.

For the good professional, obstacles are opportunities; rehearsing the obstacles to making the knowledge represented in libraries effective provides problems to be overcome and challenges for the hardy and imaginative. No intelligent reformer wants to blind himself to the obstacles; how can one remove what one cannot see? So any intelligent attempt to improve library services has to proceed from an unsentimental and realistic view of the situation in which those services are offered. From what we have so far seen in our review, it is clear enough that provision of the complete library, for unaided use and with only the presently available array of bibliographical access devices, is nothing close to an ideal solution of anyone's information problem. Under the conditions imagined, the complete library would transform almost no one's situation from undesirable to desirable.[7]

If we can accept the existence and importance of the phenomenon of studiousness in the first degree, we can quickly see that there are better ways of providing library facilities than the complete library accessible only through bibliographical works. For those of no studiousness at all,

of course, no sort of library collection is of any value as a place for search.[8]
But for those of studiousness of degree one, a collection of documents, all
linguistically and conceptually accessible, all certified as trustworthy representations of general knowledge, and all directly accessible for browsing,
not indirectly accessible through bibliographical works, and each of such
scope and character as to provide a useful source for study on a particular
sort of decision problem or concern, would be more advantageous than
the complete library that was bibliographically accessible only indirectly.
A small subcollection of the complete library, in other words, would be
as valuable, for their direct use, as the complete library itself. And indeed,
the smaller collection would be preferable to the larger one, unless the
smaller collection was conspicuously segregated within the larger one.
A collection small enough so that one could hope to find a single satisfactory
source by browsing would be preferable to a large one to which access was
indirect by way of bibliographical works, or to a large one available for
browsing but in which the components of the small collection were thinly
and randomly distributed. Only for the relatively few who were studious
to a high degree could the complete library be directly advantageous, and
even then the complete library may be less desirable than smaller partial
libraries if (as seems plausible) direct browsing is the generally preferred
means of access over indirect access through bibliographical works.[9]
For those of the first degree of studiousness, the necessity of indirect
bibliographical access might be a sufficient deterrent to prevent use of
the collection at all.

   But it is the studious of the first degree who are also the natural audience
of the commercial book store, insofar as it deals in information rather than
works of fiction and inspiration.[10] The single sources that instruct one
how to write a will, how to obtain a divorce without a lawyer, how to
invest one's money, how to purchase a house—the single-volume utilitarian
manuals—are exactly the sources stocked by the commercial book store
and exactly the sources sought by the serious but minimally studious.
Thus, the largest group of those willing to search in a library at all are
those with the best alternative sources. This is not only what one should
expect, but what is positively required to support our hypothesis of the
distribution of studiousness. Were studiousness more evenly distributed,
were there about as many who were studious in degree two as in degree
one, in degree three as in degree two, the character of the retail book trade
would be anomalous, but it is immediately intelligible if we hypothesize a

sharp break between those studious in the first degree and those studious
in higher degrees. The former constitute a sufficiently large market to
make it (just barely) profitable to provide the single-source utilitarian
manuals, and the latter constitute too small a market to be of commercial
interest except in university towns and very large cities with high concentra-
tions of professionals. What the library provides to those of modest studiousness is also provided by the commercial book stores. It is only when book
stores are lacking (as they mostly are), or only for those unable or unwilling to purchase books, that libraries are indispensable to the modestly
studious. The lack of book stores in smaller communities is consistent
with our picture of the uneven distribution of studiousness; studiousness
is so thinly distributed in the population that a community of, say, 5,000
people cannot sustain a commercial enterprise and would have no ready
source of books if there were no publicly supported communal supply.[11]

There are still many alternatives to unaided use of the complete library
with conventional bibliographic access tools that we must consider; the
provision of relatively small browsing collections is but one of the available means of increasing accessibility of information. But our reflections
so far have important implications for the rest of our discussion. Any
refinements of library service, in provision of personal assistance to library
users or provision of new and refined instruments of bibliographical access,
that have the result of easing the discovery of large or small groups of
documents that must be used together by the library patron, through
analysis, synthesis, evaluation, application to a particular problem, will
be refinements addressed only to a small fraction of the population. The
librarian can, by various means, ease the burden of search; he can increase
bibliographic accessibility and reduce the time and effort required to arrive
at documents bearing potentially useful information. But for the non-
studious, a group representing the vast majority of the population, relative
bibliographical inaccessibility is only one, and by no means the most
important, deterrent to search in document collections. Lack of studiousness itself is the first and overpowering deterrent. Unless the librarian can
find a way of simplifying the location, not of many, but of easily usable
single sources, his efforts to increase the effectiveness of the library as a
means of reducing costly ignorance are likely to benefit only the minority
willing to engage in extensive study, only those studious in the nth degree.

Who are the studious in the nth degree? Who are those prepared to
conduct searches in large collections in the expectation of having to use

together a large number of sources in relation to a single problem? They
fall mainly into three groups. First is the professional research worker
who conducts a search of "the literature" to determine the state of knowledge or the state of an art, either as an independent scholarly task (as in
the preparation of critical reviews for publication) or as an auxiliary and
preliminary study to the conduct of a piece of original research. The second
is the practicing professional looking for available knowledge to bring to
bear on a particular problem—the lawyer, doctor, engineer, policy analyst,
or legislative research worker. The third is the student, who is given the
instructional task of discovering what is revealed by some body of literature.
For any of these, search may be unavoidable and may unavoidably require
consultation and comparison of many sources. For many in the first two
categories, search may be delegated to others—a research assistant or junior
co-worker. (Those in the third category often do this work for those in
the first.) However frequent or infrequent the extended search may actually
be, the crucial fact is that it is conducted by people as part of their occupational role, exercising abilities that are part of their occupational qualifications (or, in the case of students, acquiring abilities as part of their educational aims). Studiousness in the higher degrees is expected of them, and in
virtue of their prior training, the relevant literatures are expected to be accessible to them. The time and effort required for search and for the subsequent
documentary research and application of findings are working time and
working effort, part of the job. It is those whose occupational roles require
independent analysis, evaluation, and application of the published literature
who are the primary beneficiaries of large document collections. If others
benefit, it is indirectly through the use made by these three groups.

This is not to suggest that extended search is frequent among those of
high degrees of studiousness or that high degrees of studiousness are common
among members of the three groups just singled out. While it is widely
accepted that an extended search of the literature is a proper preliminary
to any new research effort, the research worker's slowly accumulated famil-
iarity with the literature may satisfy him that search is unnecessary or
quite useless.[12] The research worker may often feel that he is already
familiar with all the relevant literature or that there is none to be found
by search: "in many fields the utility of published documents seems to be
confined almost exclusively to the communication of research results to
teachers, students, and practitioners. Thus, documents will often have
relatively little use for communication among research scholars."[13] If

teachers and professional practitioners absorb a certain amount of news
of research results from regular reading, they may still be disinclined to
undertake independent documentary research and find no occasion to do
so.[14] Extended search is as rare as the appetite and need for documentary
research. But the point remains: however infrequent extended search
actually is, it is mainly performed by or for those whose occupation requires
it and whose education has prepared them for the documentary research
to which it is a necessary preliminary.[15] Only those capable of and willing
to engage in the comparative study of documents or in documentary
research benefit directly from the availability of a research library.[16]
These are, for the most part, professional people and students. For those
of modest studiousness and less highly developed research skills, a research
library provides no direct benefit that could not be provided by a small
collection equivalent to that maintained by a good commercial book store
(of which, to be sure, there are very few), plus a collection of works of
reference too large, expensive, or infrequently needed to be parts of many
private libraries. If it is true that the larger the document collections available
to a community, the better one's information supply, and so the better one's
situation, this is not because the extensive resources are of direct benefit
to many in the community. It is, rather, because it is in the community's
interest to see that those few who are able and willing to make use of
extensive resources are given the opportunity to do so.

THE LIBRARIAN AS INFORMATION SOURCE

So far we have considered only unaided use of library collections. But
it is precisely one of the tasks of the librarian to aid people in the use of
collections, and we must now consider the sorts and amounts of aid that
are and that might be offered.

Enormous amounts of labor and skill go into the preliminary work of
organizing collections of documents and providing access instruments. This
is work that can conveniently be described as bibliographical work, since it
is, insofar as it involves knowledge and judgment rather than clerical routine,
work of the same logical character as that involved in the making of a
bibliography, an organized list of documents. Creation of a collection is
not different in principle from specifying the contents of an imaginary
collection by enumeration. Those librarians who have published catalogs

of model libraries—public libraries, junior college or college libraries, for
example—have done just what the librarian faced with the task of creating
a new library would have to do. Procurement of copies of the documents
enumerated in a model catalog, their physical preparation and handling,
and their circulation, repair, and shelving are jobs the librarian can and
often (except in the smallest libraries) does delegate to assistants within
the library or agents outside it. Deciding on the contents of a collection,
deciding on the ways in which documents are to be made discoverable by
potential users, and deciding on devices of physical arrangement and
auxiliary access instruments—these are the jobs of the librarian, and they
all have their precise analogs in the job of making a bibliography. This is
the preparatory work without which a library would be an unusable heap
of documents.

The assistance offered to library users, after the preparatory work is
done, falls into three categories: bibliographical assistance, question answering, and selection assistance.[17] Let us begin with the first of these. Librarians
offer instruction, sometimes formal but usually informal, in the use of
bibliographical access tools—catalogs, indexes, bibliographies. In varying
degrees, they themselves also use the apparatus on behalf of the library
user, preparing bibliographies or, going a step further, assembling for the
user copies of the documents corresponding to the bibliography they
prepare. This is personalized bibliographical work, and it is done on a
significant scale only in special libraries serving restricted and highly professional clienteles. One cannot expect, in a public or academic library, to
receive more than a little instruction and advice on the use of the bibliographical apparatus. Bibliographical searching is a time-consuming work,
and the amount of time that is devoted to serving any particular library
user is generally small. While the amount of assistance in the use of catalogs
and other bibliographical works that is offered must vary greatly from
library to library and from librarian to librarian, still, in general, it is
assumed that library users should be expected, and in fact prefer, to find
what they want on their own initiative, with the librarian standing ready
to give some assistance if asked to do so. But only some assistance: should
the library user pose a general problem and ask what literature there is
that might help in solving the problem, he is likely to be referred to an
appropriate section of the library shelves, or shown a bibliography, or
referred to the card catalog. He is most unlikely to be presented, after
a time, with a specially prepared bibliography, and is almost certain not to

be presented with a specially prepared report summarizing what is known that would be useful to him. That degree of personal attention is not given except under quite extraordinary circumstances or in highly specialized libraries to a carefully selected clientele. General public libraries and academic libraries are not, as presently organized and staffed, prepared to offer to do their customers' searching for them, to accept descriptions of problems and deliver lists or collections of documents containing information likely to assist in solution of the problems.

But if we are right in supposing that most people are of low degrees of studiousness, then we can suppose that librarians outside of highly specialized institutions serving professional research workers do not offer personalized bibliographical service because it is not wanted. It is not wanted by those of zero studiousness, for they do not want documents at all. It is not wanted by those of studiousness of degree one, for they do not want collections of documents requiring to be used together, compared, analyzed, and evaluated. A bibliography would be of use to them only as a means of selection of a single source, as a vehicle of recommendation. The making of extensive "demand" bibliographies is concentrated in the institutions where are found the very people who, by profession, find search unavoidable but capable of delegation. If, in fact, preparation of personalized bibliographies is not wanted by users of general purpose libraries, this is confirmation of our hypothesis that studiousness of high degrees is rare and found primarily among professional users of documents.[18]

The second sort of assistance to library users is that of question answering—the direct provision of information rather than bibliographical assistance in finding sources from which the information wanted can be derived. The vast bulk of such work is "ready-reference" work, consisting of short answers to specific factual questions, the answers discovered by the use of standard works of reference. This is fact finding, to which Wyer's description of fifty years ago still applies: "It occurs when the objective is specific, clearly stated, and the answer sought nothing more than a name, date, title, statistic, fact, or figure. It is when the question instantly suggests the right book, and the answer when found is usually in one book, often on one page. . . . In nine cases out of ten [it] can be answered from one of the half-dozen most useful reference books."[19] The librarian undertakes to answer questions insofar as direct answers can be discovered in standard sources; the librarian does not undertake to engage in computations, analyses and criticism of sources, evaluation, interpretation, inference, synthesis, application of information to particular problems. The recommended practice, indeed, is to answer by quoting from sources, identifying the source of the quotation. Paraphrasing unidentified sources and answering out of one's own knowledge are not standard professional practices. While standard professional practice does not exclude the use of nonstandard sources, primary reliance is on the use, wherever possible, of the relatively small corpus of standard reference works. Until recently, library question answering has been thought almost invariably successful, both by reference librarians and by patrons.[20] But experiments in which the same factual questions are asked of a number of different libraries have indicated that the information given is often not the best information available.[21] Wyer, in 1930, posed as a "thought question," to which he did not supply an answer, "How can a patron be made to feel that he has had the best and latest information on his subject?"[22] It appears that, in fact, the patron does not regularly get the best and latest information on his subject. Nor should this be surprising, in view of the evidence that most questions asked are answered from a few standard reference works. For a standard reference work is a dated, incomplete, more or less imperfect representation of public knowledge. The librarian could only claim that what was found in a standard reference work did represent the best and latest information on the subject on the basis of documentary research or on the basis of such knowledge as would justify the assertion that no documentary research was necessary in the particular case. But librarians do not in general claim to have, nor do they have, ability at documentary research in all the fields in which they accept and answer questions. It is not even clear that there is a general recognition of an obligation to try to determine that what the standard reference sources say represented the state of public knowledge when the sources were prepared, and that they still faithfully represent public knowledge. A book published by the American Library Association contains this remarkable comment: "One other puzzling problem in *some* questions is ascertaining that the right answer has been found." This author's view is that "the librarian's chief contribution is the discovery rather than the criticism of information," which is an odd way of saying that the librarian's job is to find answers but not to distinguish right from wrong answers, information from misinformation. On conflicting answers found in different sources, the author says, "In the final analysis, the decision as to which is right may have to be made by the expert, but the librarian can help by bringing together for comparison works by various authorities and by turning up more or less hidden sources."[23] This is not, in fact, attempted as a matter of course; reference librarians do not as a matter of routine practice look for variant answers to one question but give a single answer from a favorite standard reference work. Of course, the librarian consults sources that he supposes to be generally reliable, but he does not undertake to vouch for the accuracy of the answer on the basis of his own independent knowledge or on the basis of independent verification of the accuracy of the source in this particular case. He is not in a position to say, and does not undertake to get into the position to say, "This is the answer given in such and such a standard source, and I have every reason to believe, on the basis of my own investigation, that this answer was and still is correct." The librarian, that is, has nothing to add to the bare report that a certain source gives such and such an answer. "It is never the business of the reference librarian," says Wyer, "to determine the truth or falsity of statements found in books."[24] That is, in our terms, it is never the business of the reference librarian to say, on the basis of his own judgment, This is what is known.

The reference service offered by most libraries is thus drastically limited in two important ways: first, it is largely confined to answering specific factual questions, and second, the answering service is confined to reporting without evaluation what is contained in standard reference sources. The user who has an independent basis for trust in a particular reference source may be happy to have someone else use the source on his behalf, and those who are not overly concerned about the accuracy of the answers they receive may be happy to have a general source of answers to specific factual questions. But those who are unfamiliar with the repertory of standard sources and concerned over accuracy can be expected to be skeptical of the value of an information service whose personnel are not in a position to vouch for the accuracy of the information they give and who take no personal responsibility for the correctness of what they report. The limitation to specific factual questions is also a drastic limitation on utility. As the topical organization of catalogs and bibliographies requires that the functional questions the user would like to ask have to be translated into topical terms, so the reference service's limitation to specific factual questions imposes an analogous burden of translation. The user with a decision problem is in effect told: Tell me exactly what facts you want, and I will find them for you. But the person seeking aid in the improvement of an unsatisfactory decision situation either wants no facts at all, or does not know which facts would help. I want, let us say, to know whether there exists some alternative course of action that I have not considered; this will not count as a specific factual question to which an answer can be found in a standard reference source. Perhaps I want information that will help me clarify my own preferences among alternative actions and outcomes; this is not a specific factual question. I want to know what will be the long-range consequences of following a course of action; again, this is not a specific factual question. It is part of the conventional wisdom of librarians that patrons asking questions at a reference desk never ask for what they really want and require delicate interrogation before their true interest becomes clear.[25] But while patrons may often fail to say bluntly what they want, the librarian may add confusion by wrongly supposing that the patron really does have an acceptable specific factual question in mind that he is concealing; the librarian looks for the only sort of question he is prepared to answer.[26] Library reference service is a severely confined and unresponsible variety of information service, offering a thin surface of unevaluated "facts."

This may seem harsh; but a careful look at library reference service suggests that librarians have no basis for self-satisfaction. It is characteristic of professional judgment that it implies an assumption of personal responsibility; it may turn out to be good or bad, but it is his own personal judgment that the professional offers, and that is what we demand. But the reference librarian tries to avoid personal judgment; he avoids saying anything that would imply, "I am giving you my best judgment as to what the answer to your question is; I stand behind my answer, I accept blame if it is not right." Avoiding responsibility means avoiding professionalism; library reference service is not, by and large, a professional service.[27] How could it be? On what basis could the librarian of no more than the usual amount of general and professional education undertake to give his own judgment or expect anyone else to value it? The librarian will give answers to a question without even understanding the question or the answer, if he can find what looks, on linguistic and formal grounds, like an answer in a standard reference work. It is just as well not to claim any personal responsibility when this can happen.

The last main sort of personal assistance librarians offer is assistance in selection of particular works out of a collection, what is, or once was, called "reader's advisory service." As far as the search for information goes, such work is exactly on a par with ready reference or short-answer information service. The short-answer question is responded to with a direct quotation from a source, the long-answer question is responded to with a long text (a book, an article, or references to them). If people ask for a street address, one reads it to them from a directory. If they want to know about the French revolution, one gives them a book or shows them a collection of books. (The latter is undoubtedly much more common than the former.) Librarians are quite ready to recommend a single source of a small piece of information; they do not think of themselves as recommending, but rather as finding the answer. But they are not so ready to recommend long texts, preferring to show the patron a collection and let him make his own selection.[28] Nor is this at all difficult to understand. The librarian is not, and could not be expected to be, able to make personal recommendations on reading in general; he cannot, and is not expected to, say where accurate representations of public knowledge on all possible topics are to be found. What he can do is to produce others' recommendations—reviews, lists of recommended readings, lists of standard writings. He may be able to say, like the assistant in a book store, that one title is very popular, another has been well reviewed, and another has apparently a good scholarly reputation. Again, the librarian avoids making an independent judgment on the accuracy and trustworthiness of a text; he reports the views of others, or gives the patron a collection and lets the patron do the deciding. Ordinarily, he has no basis for an independent judgment, so it is understandable that recommendation of particular texts should play a relatively small part in library service.

It is worth dwelling on what we might call the "logical function of the book," in the information, or question-answering, aspect. Whatever may be the purposes for which books are written, their use in information service consists simply in their constituting already prepared answers to questions. Questions that arise repeatedly but unpredictably might conceivably be answered each time on an ad hoc basis; starting from the research literature, a new discourse might be composed once again explaining the theory of relativity or the reading habits of Americans. But such a pattern of behavior would be absurdly wasteful as well as slow. To prepare explanations in advance of inquiry or to prepare a variety of explanations suited to different sorts of sophistication and interest would be the reasonable plan, and if the device of the book did not exist, it would have to be invented. But it is not the physical format of the printed book that is essential; it is the fact that a certain kind of work has been done in advance of particular need and stored in some fashion that allows presentation of the results of the work on demand. For many sorts of exposition, two-dimensional visual displays are superior to the printed book, and three-dimensional displays may be of similar utility. Not the format, but the simple fact of the pre-prepared presentation is the important function of the maintenance of a collection of documents, as of the maintenance of reference collections of presentations in other formats. Collecting books, the library is collecting, among other things, already formulated responses to inquiries not yet received.

Neither in its ready-reference service nor in its recommendations on selection of documents to satisfy informational requests can the library be said to be offering an independent information service. To do so, the librarian would have to be in a position to do more than report what others say; he would have to be in a position to say on his own account what the state of public knowledge on a particular question was. Of course, anyone can do this; anyone at all can lay down the law. But not everyone deserves to be listened to, or consulted. The conditions under which one could legitimately claim to offer an information service, based on a collection of documents, are those described above (chapter one). Ability in documentary research in the area in which an answer lies is necessary, at least through the analytical stage. One who could not himself construct a representation of public knowledge could not hope to certify another's representation as faithful or unfaithful. It is true, as we have said above, that one may be in a position to say that an account cannot be adequate on the basis of research ability or knowledge of a field other than that under view. But to make a positive judgment that a representation is an accurate one, without ability to do what is necessary to construct an analogous representation oneself, is unwarranted.

Librarians refer patrons to documents for information; they can also, and sometimes do, refer patrons to other people for information. As they have directories of sources of printed information, so they have directories of human sources of information. Instead of providing documentary sources from which I can inform myself, they can refer me to agencies or individuals from whom I may be able to get advice and help. This can be a valuable service, particularly for those with an imperfect understanding of the occupational structure and the institutional arrangements for providing advice and help. Perhaps those most in need of such information are the least likely to know of, or take advantage of, a library referral service. Publicity might overcome that difficulty, at least in part, but there is a bigger difficulty. The utility of a directory service depends on its ability to make recommendations that carry some weight of trustworthiness in those cases where there are multiple independent sources to which referral might be made. If I ask to be referred to a personal information source, I do not expect to be referred to an arbitrary source, but to the best, or at least a good, source. I do not want a list, say, of doctors or lawyers; I can find that in the telephone book. I want to be told which is a good one. Even if there is only one agency or personal source for some sort of information, I want to know whether it is any good or whether I would do better to avoid it. But this sort of advice is not, so far as one can tell from published literature, offered by libraries.[29] The referral service offered is neutral and uncritical. Such service is not without value, but it is the value of a telephone directory. When one lacks a directory of one's own, it is good to have one supplied by the librarian, but selection is the problem that remains, and on this one gets no help.

Much of the foregoing is undoubtedly unfair to particular librarians and not true of information services offered in many special libraries. Many librarians are highly qualified scholars and scientists in their own right, fully prepared to accept personal responsibility for the soundness of the information they give. But these are a minority, and the usual qualifications for the position of librarian promise nothing whatever about the capacity of an individual librarian to make independent judgments on the status of the answers provided for questions or the documents recommended to supply a particular need. Particularly in small libraries, the patron may come, in the course of time, to an accurate estimate of the degree to which the librarian can be trusted as a source of accurate information; in a large library, where the same librarian may not be encountered regularly, no basis for such an estimate may be available. It is here as elsewhere in our information-gathering behavior; we prefer personal sources, and while the librarian regularly seen in a small library may become a trusted personal source, the succession of librarians seen in a large library merge into a single institutional source of unknown credibility. This single institutional source offers, in most general libraries, only a superficial and nonprofessional information source, superficial because it is based where possible on quotation from reference works and limited to small matters of "fact," nonprofessional because it is not based on any individual assumption of responsibility for the quality of the information given.

SOME IDEALS OF LIBRARY SERVICE

Let us take it as established that most of public knowledge is not accessible to most of us on the basis of unaided use of document collections, and that most of us are insufficiently studious to take advantage of what is accessible and insufficiently imaginative to make helpful applications of the portion we do discover. Let us agree that the personal services provided by librarians at present are confined to bibliographical services of most use to the studious, and rest on shallow and undependable use of standard reference works to answer a limited category of questions. Let us take it that neither the bibliographical nor the question-answering services amount to a functional information service of the sort that would discover the state of public knowledge as it bears on particular problems. If this is granted (and the last of these claims is surely undeniable), then should we not advocate that libraries institute such a service? There is no law of nature declaring that a library cannot undertake a new sort of service. If the present group of reference librarians cannot provide a functional information service, why should we not get a new group who can? An eminent library educator says that it is the library's function to "maximize the social utility of graphic records."[30] Would not a functional information service be an appropriate addition to the library's attempts to do that?

The suggestion is hardly new. One of the most ambitious statements of the ideal of the library as a general source of information is that of William S. Learned, presented in 1924. Learned proposed a community intelligence service, consisting of a collection of documents and expert intelligence personnel from whom useful information available in print could be secured "authoritatively and quickly." "The purpose of an intelligence service is first to overcome the reluctance people have to seeking information, and later to maintain their interest and support by supplying just the information needed in the form in which it can best be utilized by the person in question and in a manner that invites repetition. This is a task for an expert possessing personal tact, quick intellectual sympathies and appreciation, a thorough knowledge of a certain field of material, precision and discrimination of thought, and the power promptly to organize results." A true community intelligence service is not passive, but active and aggressive: "its business is not only to answer but to raise educative questions in as many minds as possible; it must not only interpret the dream, but for many persons it must provide the dream as well."

Learned does not make it quite clear just what the information personnel
are to do. At first, it appears that their job would be a simply bibliographical
one, distributing notices of publications that are aimed at "adapting important knowledge to special types of users" and have been produced by others
as part of a general effort toward "revising the whole field of communicable
knowledge with a view to its effective consumption." The bibliographical
job appears to be necessary since "most of this product trickles through
publishers' notices, book reviews, news items, and into libraries and title-
lists where, for lack of a suitable distributing medium, it soon lies smothered
and useless so far as the great majority of the population are concerned.
Meanwhile, the questions that it could answer, the ambitions and struggles
that it could promote and assist, the unrecognized needs and opportunities
that it could reveal are teeming in the minds of men who either know no
recourse for satisfaction, or have no time for a laborious search. The daily
losses in energy and material that result from sheer ignorance on the part
of otherwise intelligent persons of how to avail themselves of the contents
of books must be colossal beyond all calculation." This is obviously costly
ignorance in our sense, and the remedy is for the community intelligence
service to furnish, on request or on their own initiative, bibliographical
information about publications containing useful information. But something more than a functional reorganization and dissemination of bibliographical information seems to be meant. At the least, estimates of the
specific value of publications are to be provided, and at the most, the
available knowledge is to be reorganized, simplified, and presented in new
ways.[31] Still, despite discussions of lectures, moving pictures, and so on,
documents already prepared by others are the center of Learned's concern,
and the diffusion of bibliographical information is his chief proposal.

Let us go beyond Learned's proposal. Let us propose a true information
service, one that would be based on the performance of documentary
research aimed at discovering the state of public knowledge where it has
not so far been explicitly summarized, and at evaluating existing summaries
in terms of their present accuracy, and one that would try to capture some
of the utility of knowledge for the solution of particular problems. Such a
service would accept inquiries in the form of statements of a problem
and respond with a description of what is presently known that bears on
solution of the problem. It would explicitly undertake to vouch for the
accuracy of the information given as being part of public knowledge, and
would deliberately attempt to provide only such information as was of

probable utility in the solution of a problem or the improvement of a
decision situation. This may be what Learned was actually proposing;
in any case, it is worth taking seriously as a proposal for the more effective
utilization of knowledge.

We must be careful to say where we are proposing such a service be
offered. Learned proposed that his intelligence services be located in
public libraries, and it is almost inevitable that we should do so as well.
The libraries maintained by and for commercial, industrial, and professional organizations, and those serving primarily the interests and needs
of educational and research institutions, will be provided with such information services as the institutions served can be persuaded are worth their
cost. It would do us little good to confect reasons why an industrial
organization that maintains no research staff at all should begin to do so.
Neither would it be useful to invent reasons why its research staff should
include a specialist in documentary research, or, if there is to be such a
specialist, why he should be a member of the library staff rather than of
the research staff. What is advantageous in one sort of industrial or business
environment would be useless and wasteful in another, and we may leave
it to the managers to discover where their greatest advantage lies. Nor is it
likely to be illuminating to argue for adding documentary research specialists to the staffs of educational and research institutions, whose members
are presumed already capable of doing such work themselves. For the
general question, of which this would be a special subpart, would be the
question of how far it is desirable to provide research assistants to research
workers; the institutional location of the assistants would be of subordinate
interest. We cannot hope to say anything on the general question of optimal
policies on research in institutional settings, but we may manage to clarify
the question of information services outside such settings. Our concern
should not be with the provision of services that would substitute for
those that could be and sometimes are conducted in institutional settings;
we should not concern ourselves with the question whether a public
agency should, for instance, perform documentary research for business
firms or whether an independent professional who finds it too time-
consuming to conduct his own documentary research should be provided
with a public assistant. These are serious questions but have to be left
unanswered. Our interest is not whether more, and public, assistance
should be given to those who are already able to help themselves to the
contents of the stock of public knowledge, but whether assistance should

be given to those who are not able, which is a question of increasing the accessibility of public knowledge rather than of relieving those to whom it is already accessible of some of the burdens of access.

Again, we are not considering the desirability of constructing the net-work of information analysis centers, organized on a disciplinary basis, that was discussed at the end of chapter one. The purpose of such centers is not to apply public knowledge to individual problems, but to create and maintain up to date a representation of public knowledge in some particular area of inquiry. The service we are interested in is a service of a functionally oriented character, falling into the supplementary group of agencies described in the first chapter. We there alluded to professional schools as examples of such second-level agencies; we will now consider a further, local service, not as part of a formal educational program, but as a direct service to private individuals. We are interested in the reduction of costly ignorance by the provision of documentary research services available, as are the services of the public library, to anyone in a community, and we might as well propose that the services be offered through the public library, it being a natural if not the only possible agency through which to offer the service.

What kind and amount of service could be provided? Suppose I presented my problem about deciding whether to rely exclusively on public transporta-tion. Would the research staff study the available documents and prepare for me a detailed report on the state of knowledge as it bears on my personal problem? This is the sort of thing that might be done once—for a legislative agency, for example—but we could not seriously propose that a new public library agency be created to write a book to order for any individual who requested it. To be even momentarily plausible, the service would have to be restricted, for example, to the performance of extensive research tasks only for a small favored clientele (such as public decision makers) or to the performance of small research tasks. Since our interest is in helping those who do not themselves have the capacity to do documentary research or the resources to hire their own research staffs, let us assume that the second limitation must be enforced: whatever service is given must not require lengthy research or the preparation of large individualized reports. We must concentrate on costly ignorance remediable by relatively small amounts of expert effort at documentary research.

It is immediately apparent, however, that if we propose to bring about a reduction of costly ignorance, we are choosing a most unpromising agency

in the documentary research service which people may consult when they
feel like it. For we have no reason to suppose that people are aware of
what it is they need to know, and we have no reason to expect that dissatisfaction will drive them to use the service. We had better think first
in terms of an agent whose job it is to discover or diagnose costly ignorance,
and we should think next of a means of bringing the needed information
to people's attention directly through some active medium of communication, not indirectly through the dissemination of bibliographical notices.
It was odd that Learned should have described his community intelligence
service under the heading of "diffusion of knowledge"; an agency that
disseminates bibliographical information and that answers such questions
as are put to it is not likely to achieve much in the way of the diffusion of
knowledge. The mass media, the specialized media, personal "change
agents," and the educational system, all are better agents of diffusion.[32]
If no suitable publication media exist, then it would make sense to encourage
their creation. Insertion of new information and reinsertion of overlooked
or forgotten old information into established communications channels,
and the creation of new channels as carriers of new sorts of information
are the relatively fast means of diffusion. Change of the content of educational curricula, creating new devices and arrangements for continuing
education, are slower but of equal significance. If we discover that every-
body or some or all members of an identifiable group of people are ignorant
of some things they need to know, then we should try to see that the information is inserted into communication channels already aimed at the
appropriate audience.[33] Creation of new channels where no existing channel
is available is a far less satisfactory means of diffusion, since any new
channel must compete for attention with all the old ones and will not be
added to the information systems of those who are relatively satisfied with
their information supply. In any case, while a library-based documentary
research service might be a suitable agency to discover such needed information, it is not obvious that the task of broadcasting the information, of
inserting it into appropriate communication channels, is one that fits comfortably or logically into the context of a documentary research service.

These considerations bear on the form, not on the content, of diffusion; we have said nothing of what sort of information it might be that
a documentary research service might find to be lacking to, and needed
by, everyone or the members of some particular group. But we shall not
now approach this question; it will arise again shortly. For whether or not

we undertake to inform whole populations of things they need to know, our functional information service must certainly also respond to individual needs. Whether or not we try to supply what masses and groups need all at once, we must also be concerned with the irregular and unpredictable information needs of individuals. We want, in the first place, to increase the accessibility of public knowledge to individuals.

Or is that really the proper goal? Let us return to the notion of availability, with which we began this chapter. There are two quite distinct ways in which we can make knowledge (not documents) available: we can offer opportunities for a person to acquire it or else we can offer the help of those who already have it. At first it may sound strange to say that legal or medical knowledge is available to me in the person of my lawyer or doctor. It is undeniably true that I learn little or no law or medicine by asking my lawyer or doctor for help. But I have the use of their knowledge, and as far as I am concerned, that is as good as, or better than, knowing myself what they know. For they take on the burden of learning and applying the things there are to know. Though I would like to know all they know, I would not like to go to the trouble of acquiring it. As it is, their knowledge is not accessible to me: I cannot understand and I cannot critically evaluate the things they would tell me if they set out to recite all they know. But though it is inaccessible, it is available, for I have the use of it, in that they will themselves use it on my behalf.

If we admit the two ways of making knowledge available, then the question before us becomes: Do we care more about increasing opportunities for people to acquire knowledge or about increasing the amount they have at their disposal, the amount they have the use of? But this in turn becomes the question: Do we really want an information service? For the information service offers to tell me what is known that relates to a problem so that I may come to have the knowledge myself and use it as I may. The advisory service, on the other hand, may be willing to explain the things on which the advice given depends, but it is prepared to go much further, by applying things known to the circumstances of my case and recommending courses of action.

Common sense, as well as the preceding discussion, argue in favor of the advisory method.[34] Here is an elderly person with a small capital fund, being courted by unscrupulous men urging unwise investments. Shall we offer a course in finance? Or shall we offer an impartial and informed public adviser? Does the elderly person really have, at this late date, to

learn all that one needs to know to manage investments? Can we offer
nothing more comfortable than a course of instruction? There is a mother
worried about the eating habits of her children. Shall we offer the latest
findings of biochemistry? Or shall we offer advice on diets? Offer both,
by all means, but remember that the advice may be welcome to many for
whom a course of instruction would be weary work.

It is not hard for a sympathetic person to become convinced that society
offers too little in the way of easy avenues to trustworthy advisers. (*Ease*
and *trust* are both crucial terms.) Nor is it difficult to see that the only
way in which large specialized bodies of knowledge are in fact going to be
brought to bear on the solution of practical problems is, for most adults,
by the provision of advisers. Even when we have the ability, the time and
effort required for prolonged study are unacceptably great. But prolonged
study is just what would be required to develop the background against
which the information provided by a documentary research service would
be intelligible and could be utilized. If knowledge really could be acquired
in isolated pieces whose comprehension and utilization required no prior
learning, provision of an information service would be an attractive goal.
But a documentary information service, while it would lift the burden of
documentary research from the seeker after knowledge, would not waive
the requirement of study to achieve comprehension. To draw one's own
conclusions about the best course of action on the basis of information
provided by such a service would still require the effort of study—unless
nothing more than familiar common sense matters were involved. Whether
the documentary information service presents us with a textbook guaranteed
to be sound or with hitherto unformulated public knowledge intelligible
only in the light of prior mastery of textbook knowledge, study will be
required, and the application in practice of the results of study will be
risky. There is no way in which we can acquire knowledge without effort.
If we cannot or will not make the effort, then the only way in which we
can have the advantage of knowledge is by taking advice rather than
instruction.

So let us grant that an advisory service is likely to be more effective
than an information service in achieving the greater utilization of knowledge and remedying costly ignorance. But in that case, why propose that
the service be offered through a library? The only reason for basing an
advisory service on a library would be that it essentially requires what the
library has, a document collection, or what the librarians have, bibliographi-

cal expertise. If we propose, however, to increase the availability and accessibility of professional advisers, there is no apparent reason that the professional adviser should become part of a library staff. Professionals need documents in varying degrees, and so library resources must be available to them. But there is no reason why a new public financial adviser, or a new public medical adviser, should be on the staff of a library. It could turn out to be advantageous to provide a documentary research service, not to members of the public, but to the public advisers, and such a service could well be a library staff function. But advisers who dealt directly with the members of the public they served would have no particular interest in, or need for, a place on the library staff.

This assumes that the public advisers will advise in areas in which special new investigations into the state of knowledge are exceptional rather than routine, for if they were routine, then the advisory service could be considered to be essentially dependent on research collections of documents, while if they are exceptional, the service need only have access to research collections for sporadic use. This is true, in fact, of the common practice of the recognized professions and near-professions; one does not expect that a completely new investigation into the state of knowledge will be needed to solve the ordinary problems brought to the professional. But we have not yet definitely said what are the areas in which public advisers are needed; perhaps they are not areas for the already recognized professions and near-professions at all. On what matters is advice needed by ordinary people, and who is able to provide the advice needed? The answers are really not in doubt. People's concerns, their most important and difficult problems, center around their own well-being and that of their families and friends—physical and mental health, economic security, legal problems, the education of children, and the like. Lawyers and doctors will insist on appropriate qualifications for any public advisers in their areas. Financial and educational counselors are not so well organized, but the institution of public advisers in such areas would require the establishment of appropriate professional qualifications—which would certainly not be simply bibliographical qualifications. We are indeed proposing a corps of professionals as public advisers, of different qualifications from those of librarians.

The new or expanded array of public advisers would logically qualify as the agents for the job of discovering and formulating what was information generally needed by whole populations and groups; we thus return to the question earlier posed about the content of diffusion. For those actively

engaged in advising on particular problems are better situated than those
not so engaged for discovering the prevalent gaps in common knowledge.
Thus, the main functions to be served by our original proposal are taken
over by a group of professional advisers outside the library. But this result
was indeed implicit at the beginning. For if we set ourselves the goal of
adding experts at documentary research to the library staff, we could not
have supposed that anyone could be expert at documentary research in
general. We argued, in chapter one, that the competent documentary
researcher must be a competent practitioner in the area of his research
interest. The surveyor of knowledge must be a member of the group responsible for cultivation of the particular area of knowledge surveyed. It has
repeatedly been recognized that library "subject specialists" must have
advanced qualifications in the fields of their specialties. When we proposed
to offer documentary research service, we were committing ourselves to
the addition to library staffs of, not one, but as many professionally qualified people as there are fields within which we expected to offer information. Learned, indeed, thought that a staff of at least a score of experts
might be reasonable for the library of a city of 200,000.[35] Surely, that
number is too small to provide expert information service over the whole
field of knowledge, though the same number of public advisers would be
more nearly satisfactory. But when we committed ourselves to adding a
corps of professionals to library staff, we opened ourselves directly to the
question: Why limit them to giving information when it is advice that is
wanted? Then, lacking an answer, we lost any semblance of a rationale
for adding the corps of experts to the library staff at all, rather than simply
adding them to the larger corps of public servants, unless, indeed, we
proposed to add experts who were not very expert and were not capable
of giving advice. But why prefer not very expert informants on a library
staff to expert advisers in other public offices?

Still we may ask if the range of professions is complete, if there are no
gaps in the array of occupations that utilize bodies of knowledge to solve,
or recommend solutions for, problems of choice. If there are gaps, may
there not be gaps that would be best filled by specialists in the utilization
of documents? Is there no room for an "information professional" with
more than bibliographical expertise, but distinct from the already existing
range of professions and near-professions? Of course, the answer must be
yes; new professions arise regularly, and one would be foolhardy to try to
say what new occupational groups will and will not come into existence.

But let us see if we can describe, very tentatively and sketchily, the sorts of new information professionals that might occupy the interstices in the present array of professions. To do so, let us return to the notion of the personal information system.

Personal information systems may be inadequate in particular cases or inefficient in general. An individual might want two sorts of advice: advice on a particular decision problem for which his information system had inadequately prepared him, or advice on the reorganization of the information system in part or as a whole. In the first case, what is wanted is not the help of an information system specialist but the help of a specialist in the area of the decision—law, health, education, or money. Once that problem is solved, a new problem might be addressed, namely, how to alter one's information system so as to be prepared for similar future problems, and on this, the advice of a personal information system specialist, if there were such people, would be useful. In both sorts of case, simple bibliographical assistance can be helpful; in neither sort of case is bibliographical assistance the only or the best kind of help. A general information system specialist would by no means be concerned only or primarily with arranging document supplies. It is hard to imagine designing, or systematically correcting, an information system without analyzing and designing or redesigning procedures for decision. Information systems are maintained to guide decision and action, and we may need less information but better procedures for using the information we already have and get. The knowledge required for the design of procedures for decision, and that required for designing ways of collecting the information required in the application of those procedures, is far from the bibliographical expertise librarians have, from the documentary research ability of the new library service proposed above, and from the new array of public advisers. Such a new profession does not look like a simple extension of the present practice of librarianship.

What it does sound like is a general "technology of decision"; it does sound like what has been called an "intellectual technology," or an "operative technology."[36] The theoretical basis for such a technology would be furnished by normative theories of decision, theories of how decisions ought to be made, which include, as a subpart, theories of how to decide when information should be gathered and how it should be used. Since information is wanted for the sake of decision, the kind and amount of information to be acquired cannot be decided independently of choice of procedures to be followed in making the decisions. This is true even though the relevance of information to a decision situation can in theory be determined independently of knowledge of exact procedures for decision. The design of decision procedures is in part just this, to decide *which* relevant information to take into account and to decide *what* information to seek and use, given the facts that search is costly and imperfect and that use may be difficult and time-consuming. The design of decision procedures is in part a matter of deciding what relevant information to ignore. But it is also a matter of deciding what needs to be decided, and knowledge of the relevance of information to a decision problem does not give one knowledge that one is addressing the right problem. Fragments of such a technology of decision already exist under names like systems analysis, operations research, and management science.[37] There seems no reason to doubt that more fragments will continue to be developed. The technology could easily become complex enough to produce a division of labor and the creation of specialties in information analysis (if indeed they have not already occurred).[38] But a normative technology of information, that is, a technology of the choice of the best patterns of information gathering and information use, would be part of a more general normative technology of decision. The best patterns of information gathering would be specified by reference to uses to be made, and specifying use would be specifying, entirely or in part, the decision procedures to be followed.[39]

We can indeed describe another imaginary professional—let us call him the information doctor, for reasons that will be apparent—who does not try to prescribe new procedures for making decisions, but who tries to predict the effect on decisions of different sorts of information systems. The information doctor aims, like the decision technologist, at making prescriptions, at recommending effective techniques for attaining one's goals. But, unlike the decision technologist, the information doctor goes on the assumption that decisions will continue to be made in the same ways as before his "treatment," and he tries to select a pattern of information flow that will lead to improvements in the decisions made in those same old ways. This may sound easy enough until one reflects on the variety of ways in which information enters into decisions (see, in chapter two, "Knowledge and Decision"). The information doctor does not tell his client how information should be used; he simply tries to predict that, if a particular sort of information system (pattern of information sources) is used, decisions will improve. In effect, he tries to put himself in a posi-

tion to be able to say, Take this, and you'll find that good things happen
to you. No one is now in such a position, and it is not certain that anyone
will ever be in such a position. The psychological basis for the information
doctor's practice does not now and may never exist. For we do not know
that we will ever be able to relate patterns of information intake with
quality of decisional outcome; we lack a basis for connecting means
(patterns of information sources) with ends (improvement of decisions
without prescription of decision-making procedures).

The information doctor may never exist; the technologist of decision
already exists, though only modestly equipped. Both could claim the title
of information professional; neither seems likely to practice in a library
setting, since, to repeat, documentary sources are by no means the most
important information sources that either would have to consider. Concern
for the proper design of personal information systems is only in some part
a concern for documents.

The proposal to add documentary research specialists to public library
staffs reflects one ideal of library service, that it not only provide the
materials from which what is known about the world can be discovered,
but that it provide a staff to do the work of discovery as well. The proposal
to add new professional information specialists to library staffs reflects
another ideal, that librarians should become the general experts, not simply
on document supply systems, but on information-gathering systems generally.
There is a third proposal to consider, namely, that librarians should aim to
improve on the performance of the bibliographical services that are already
their responsibility. As specialist in bibliography, the librarian has two jobs:
to assist in the discovery of documents of potential use, and to facilitate
physical access to such documents. These can be conveniently described
as the *discovery* and the *delivery* functions. They are logically distinct,
though in the process of discovering documents by browsing, they are in
fact simultaneously performed, which goes a long way toward explaining
the attractions of browsing. The librarian's first and most important job
is the preliminary one of creating and maintaining collections and arrangements for access to documents in other collections, and for providing
means of bibliographical access to materials wherever located. Next in
importance is bibliographical assistance to library users, from general
instruction to highly specialized individual assistance. In neither the preliminary work nor the work of direct assistance to library users, and in
neither the discovery nor the delivery aspect of the work can librarians

claim to have reached the limits of their effectiveness. The direction in which improvement lies is not in doubt: it is that of easing the burden of discovery and of physical access to documents. There is plenty of room for improvement in service in both departments. Those who approach libraries wanting specific documents of which they have (complete or incomplete, accurate or inaccurate) bibliographical descriptions often encounter barriers to access that could be lifted and delays in time that could be reduced. Those who must search for materials are faced with bibliographical access tools—catalogs and indexes—whose cumbersomeness, complexity, and inconvenience are often positive deterrents to library use. Instruction in the use of access tools and reference works, which should be part of every undergraduate education and available to everyone, has not yet been systematically and successfully developed or encouraged. Librarians have not exhausted the possibilities of their service as regular sources of bibliographical information, particularly in the direction of assistance to those concerned with the reorganization and application of existing knowledge. There are still untried possibilities of service through the undertaking of continuous or occasional search not for familiar but for unfamiliar sorts of material, not for obviously related but for unobviously related materials, and not for the easy but for the hard to find materials. This implies sustained and personal connections between librarian and document user, not impersonal and institutionalized service. It also implies a degree of independence and adventuresomeness of service that has hitherto not been general. Whether librarians can develop demonstrably useful personalized bibliographical services of this sort further than they have already been taken, or whether their principal role will continue to be in the maintenance of physical and bibliographical access systems for largely unaided use by patrons, a reorientation toward the functional, rather than topical or disciplinary, organization of document supplies represents a possible goal for future development, one that explicitly recognizes the primacy of the need to bring knowledge to the point of use. This is the ideal of library service as bibliography in aid of the reorganization and application of knowledge.

If we were to accept this ideal as the proper one for the future development of library service, what place would we assign to the traditional reference service, so severely criticized above? The first rule would be, not to misrepresent the service. If the librarian is not in a position to vouch for the accuracy of information given in response to inquiries, this should be made clear to the inquirer. No claims should be made that library reference services are general sources of reliable information. The exact role of each librarian and the individual librarian's qualifications for undertaking such work should be made known to the would-be user of the service. Sophisticated people are probably not often deluded about the character of library reference services, but naïve people may often be. It should be recognized as a responsibility of the librarian to inform the naïve of the limitations of the assistance that is offered, and of the fact (when it is a fact) that the librarian is not in a position independently to judge the quality of the information given. This caution might lead to less frequent use of library reference service, which might be a benefit, since the time thus freed could be devoted to bibliographical assistance of the sort the librarian can claim special ability to give.

Emphasis on the bibliographical character of the librarian's work does not imply an exclusive concern for printed materials as opposed to graphic and aural records, but it does imply a primary concern for records, for information-bearing objects. The librarian is not a specialist in information in general, but in information about records. The librarian's job is a job of management of information-bearing objects, and the continually improved performance of that necessary job is a natural and reasonable goal for the future.[40]

LIBRARIES AND PUBLIC KNOWLEDGE

That the stock of public knowledge is, and should be treated as, a common possession, the use and benefits of which should be available not to a restricted few but to mankind generally, is a plausible axiom for information policy. Knowledge should be available to all, and the more needed, the more readily available. This is unexceptionable as a general goal, except to those who prefer that the populace remain in a salutory state of ignorance. If one made knowledge available for use by making documents available for use, the librarian's role in achieving the goals of such a policy would be clear-cut, for there is little obscurity in the notion of making a document available to a person. But the availability of knowledge is not like the availability of an object—a book, a hammer, or a loaf of bread. One cannot put knowledge into another's hands or into a mind. We can in theory make the whole world's supply of documents available on easy terms; only technical difficulties and lack of money, not theoretical difficulties, prevent us from doing so. But we do not make knowledge available simply by making available documents in which knowledge is represented. It is safe to predict flatly that even the instant availability of every document in the world to everyone would not significantly alter the quality of decisions in a noticeable fraction of instances. Universal physical access to documents is a librarian's ideal, but not an ideal with much attraction for anyone else. No more is universal bibliographical access, if that is understood in the sense of an ability to discover everything ever published that fits some topical description, such as everything ever written about the dolphin, or every document that mentions dolphins. But suppose, instead, we think of an ideal system that would provide a steady flow of documents of high probable utility which magically arrived well in advance of each decision that an individual was going to face: would not such a functionally oriented system be of incalculable value? Conceivably, but such a flow of documents would be, from the individual's point of view, simply another, competing, flow in his private information system. Whether it was welcomed and used, or rejected, would depend on whether it yielded more useful information at no more cost in time and effort than did other sources previously utilized. To those who already had what they considered a relatively satisfactory information supply, the additional document supply would be of no advantage. To those with what they considered an unsatisfactory information supply, it might be an advantage, provided it was accurately adjusted to their capacities for understanding and using the contents, and to their willingness to devote time and energy to the attempt. Such an accurate adjustment of document supply to information appetite would be truly miraculous.

As long as we are imagining miracles, let us imagine another. A supply of expert advisers, one or more of whom appeared like a genie just when a decision had to be made and offered appropriate advice, would for most of us be a yet more dazzlingly advantageous service (as long as they did not intrude when not wanted). This would be due not to an ignoble lack of curiosity or preference for ignorance, but to a preference for the avoidance of unnecessary work. The collection of information and its mastery and application in decision making are simply means to the end of a satisfactory life situation; if we can attain the end without effort, we will do so.

Librarians, like other enthusiastic purveyors of merchandise, like to think of the good it would do if everyone sought their wares, but they think only of the benefits (which they see obscurely), and not of the costs. They imagine, not the process of acquisition of knowledge, but the condition of its possession; they imagine what it would be like to have, not to acquire, the knowledge they think they have to offer. The would-be buyers are in a very different position; not having the knowledge, they cannot see what its possession would be like, but they suspect, correctly, that one does not get it for nothing. Not having unlimited resources to spend or unlimited demands to be met, they use libraries, not as much as librarians would wish, but as little as they can.

The fantasy of a functionally oriented automatic document supply usefully illustrates the narrow limits within which librarians can maneuver in their attempts to help in the utilization of knowledge and the reduction of costly ignorance. On one side, the character of the existing supply of documents (the world's total supply, not the collection that any library happens to have) sets a limit. What libraries have to offer depends on what others have published; libraries are not themselves independent originators of knowledge or of presentations of knowledge. In many cases, the document supply contains nothing of use—nothing known, nothing made public, or nothing accessible (linguistically, conceptually, critically) to the user. On the other side, the limits are set by the preferences, habits, abilities, and resources of the potential user. The library cannot supply time or ability if it is lacking. It can provide documents to study, but not the inclination to study. It cannot make it more economical to acquire a body of knowledge through study than to draw on the advice of someone who already has the knowledge. It cannot do much, if anything at all, to create dissatisfaction in those who are relatively satisfied with an information supply, however large or small, that is independent of library use. (Should it try?) What it can do is provide easy access to documents, but easier access will be most appreciated by those who cannot avoid being large users of documents. It is not the difficulty of access, but the time, effort, and difficulty of using documents that are the major deterrents to library use.[41]

This sounds, and in part surely is, a fairly superficial matter, merely a perhaps temporary or local penchant for economizing in the use of information. But there is a deeper limitation on the efficacy of library services in making knowledge available that would remain however much our appetites for information increased and however little we counted costs of time and effort. J. Robert Oppenheimer, in a lecture given in 1958 at Vassar College, spoke movingly of the imbalance "between what is known to us as a community, what we can all take for granted in each other, and what is known somehow by man, but not by men. . . . Mature men today—and this is true whatever their status—are really deeply and necessarily quite unaware of the greater part of human knowledge . . . . most of the new knowledge is specialized in character. It is not something that you can understand if you have spent all your life in a normal commonsense life, or even in a rather abnormal one. . . . That is why the core of our cognitive life has this sense of emptiness. It is because we learn of learning as we learn of something remote, not concerning us, going on on a distant frontier."[42] What is stinging about this is not our actual ignorance of most of human knowledge, but our inevitable ignorance. It is not that human knowledge is unavailable to us because the documents in which it is explicitly or implicitly represented are not available to us; rather, it is that public knowledge is no longer directly accessible to us at all. With the best supply of documents in the world, we would still lack the ability to come to know what is known.

Our earlier arguments concluded that, first, large research collections are of direct benefit only to the relatively few people capable of documentary research and willing to engage in it, and that, second, the best and indeed the only practical way of making large bodies of specialized knowledge available to most people is by making available the services of expert, knowledgeable advisers. These are simply two aspects of the same phenomenon, of the relative inaccessibility of the knowledge represented in the document supply. The social division of labor in the production and utilization of knowledge both encourages the development of an ever more remote supply of knowledge and provides a way of partially overcoming that remoteness because it both leads to the concentration of knowledge in various occupational specialties and makes the increasing stock of knowledge available in the persons of the specialists. Intensive use of large document collections is made primarily by some members of the occupational specialties in the production and utilization of knowledge, and the pattern of the library system largely reflects the pattern of occupational specialization. When one ignores the complex relation between the stock of knowledge and the stock of documents, and the enormous work required to get knowledge for oneself out of the stock, it might appear that simply providing more documents to more people would be a means of equalizing the unequal distribution of knowledge and allowing the whole stock of knowledge, or all the public and usable portion, to be brought to bear on private decision making. But the uneven distribution of knowledge in the adult population has causes that are entirely independent of the uneven availability of documents and too deep to be perceptibly influenced by a change in the conditions of availability of documents.

Do we have to conclude, then, that libraries have no significant part to play in the social arrangements for reducing costly ignorance? By no means. The main present function of the library system is as part of and adjunct to the educational system. Most librarians in elementary and secondary schools, college and university libraries serve primarily students and their teachers, and a large part of the use of public libraries is made by students in connection with formal educational programs. By deliberately confining our attention to the information seeking of adults out of school, we set aside the largest and most important part of the actual library audience. The educational system is society's main arrangement for reducing costly ignorance, and libraries are an indispensable element in that complex of teachers and educational artifacts. Once past the period of formal schooling, it is principally those whose occupational function is the search for new knowledge or the application of complex bodies of old knowledge to whom the library is an essential information source, and their main reliance is on the array of special libraries as well as on college and university libraries. Libraries serve the reduction of costly ignorance, then in the assistance they provide to the process of formal education and in the direct assistance they give to the occupational specialists in knowledge, direct benefit to whom is indirect benefit to all to whom their knowledge is available.[43] And this is no small service.

Finally, we must return to the question of the use of public knowledge, not to balance our story, for we have deliberately chosen imbalance, but to gesture toward the necessary counterbalance. Public knowledge, we said, is not merely for contemplation and admiration; it is for use. But this aggressively pragmatic view is one-sided. As has been noted, much of what is known is of no imaginable use except to the scholar or scientist whose aim is to discover more knowledge. Scholars and scientists tend, in one mood, to stress the practical benefits of their work—the unpredictable future benefits of scientific discovery, the improvement in the quality of life from study of the past, and so on. But in another mood they will stress the value of knowledge for its own sake—its intrinsic value, irrespective of practical uses and the effects of acquiring it. Both views are in fact defensible. Knowledge sought for its own sake does turn out, from time to time, to have unexpected practical applications. But the pursuit of knowledge can also be seen as part of high culture, as a continual work on the creation of a cultural object with as much claim to intrinsic value as any work of art. The body of public knowledge can in fact be viewed as a supremely complex work of art, and it is not by accident that scientists talk of the beauty of their findings. In our attempt to get clear about the library as a source of information useful in decision making, we put aside the other service of the library as a source of what is simply of interest. No condescension toward the satisfaction of interests was meant. There is a strong connection between the satisfaction of interests and aesthetic satisfaction, a connection that was barely hinted at in the comparison of concerns and interests in chapter two, but which could be developed at some length. A library that houses a representation of public knowledge houses a representation of our single most complex cultural artifact, our thing of highest intellectual achievement. There is a case to be made, though we will let others make it, for the claim that this thing should be made available to everyone, whether or not he chooses to examine it and whether or not he can grasp much of it. The case might rest not on the utility of knowledge but on the intrinsic value of the satisfaction of interests, of knowing more about the world, as the case for symphony orchestras or art museums rests not on utility but on the intrinsic value of the satisfactions they afford. When we count up the benefits provided by the library system, there is more to be counted than the improvements in decisions and the applications of knowledge to the solution of practical problems; there is also the consideration of the value of making available, for whoever may want to enjoy it, our most important cultural object.

CHAPTER 1

1. This is true of scholars and scientists, but not of technologists; see Derek J. De Solla Price, "The Scientific Foundations of Science Policy," *Nature* 206 (17 Apr. 1965): 236: "Those who think they want to read—though the documents were not written for them—are the technologists who feel they should look for useful knowledge to apply. But the technologists, though they want to read, do not want to publish—they want to produce artefacts and processes. This is perhaps the paradoxical conflict which has made much noise over an information crisis." On the importance of publication for scientists, see John Ziman, *Public Knowledge: An Essay Concerning the Social Dimension of Science* (Cambridge: Cambridge Univ. Press, 1968), ch. 6 et passim.

2. "Address by the Right Hon. Lord Rayleigh," *Report of the Fifty-Fourth Meeting of the British Association for the Advancement of Science; Held at Montreal in August and September 1884* (London: John Murray, 1885), p. 20.

3. J. D. Bernal, *The Social Function of Science* (London: Routledge, 1939), p. 118.

4. Lewis M. Branscomb, "Is the Literature Worth Reviewing?" *Scientific Research,* 27 May 1968, p. 50. See Philip M. Boffey, "Scientific Data: 50 Pct. Unusable?" *Chronicle of Higher Education,* 24 Feb. 1975, pp. 1, 6, for similar comments by his successor as director of the National Bureau of Standards. See also Gertrude London, "The Publication Inflation," *American Documentation* 19 (Apr. 1968): 137-141.

5. This is one strong reason for resisting the claim that citation counts, that is, counts of the frequency with which a piece of scientific work is referred to in subsequent publications, are an adequate measure of the value of scientific work. See Jonathan R. Cole and Stephen Cole, *Social Stratification in Science* (Chicago: University of Chicago Press, 1973), for a particularly strong defense of citation counts as a measure of value.

6. That science is public knowledge, and vice versa, is exactly Ziman's argument in *Public Knowledge.*

7. "It is a ridiculous, but commonly held, belief that the publication of the results of particular investigations is sufficient to create a body of knowledge. . . . The job of the review writer is to sift and sort the primary observations and to delineate this larger pattern . . . . It is only by such public re-appraisals that those who are not already expert in the subject can have any idea of the credibility of the innumerable results 'reported in the literature' " (John Ziman, "Information, Communication, Knowledge," *Nature* 224 [25 Oct. 1969] : 323).

8. *Science, Government, and Information: A Report of the President's Science Advisory Committee* (Washington, D.C.: Government Printing Office, 1963), p. 33; Herman M. Weisman, *Information Systems, Services, and Centers* (New York: Becker and Hayes, 1972), pp. 138-139, 143.

9. Cf. Allan Mazur, "Disputes Between Experts," *Minerva* 11 (Apr. 1973): 243-262.

10. The "knowledge occupations" are not to be confused with the "knowledge industries" described by Fritz Machlup in *The Production and Distribution of Knowledge in the United States* (Princeton: Princeton Univ. Press, 1962): "A chemical engineer employed in the food industry, a designer in the shoe industry, an accountant or a lawyer in the chemical industry, all are engaged in the production of knowledge according to their *occupation,* but not according to the *industry* in which they work. On the other hand, a janitor in a school building, a charwoman in a research laboratory, a mechanic in a television studio, all are engaged in the production of knowledge according to the *industry* in which they work, but not according to their *occupation"* (p. 45). Machlup includes many more occupations (and industries) in the category of knowledge-producing than I would.

11. That scientists have special methods of inquiry is described as a fairy tale by the philosopher Paul Feyerabend in " 'Science,' The Myth and Its Role in Society," *Inquiry* 18 (Summer 1975): 167-181.

12. Norman Storer and Talcott Parsons, "The Disciplines as a Differentiating Force," in Edward B. Montgomery, ed., *The Foundations of Access to Knowledge: A Symposium* (Syracuse: Syracuse University, 1968), pp. 101-121; Talcott Parsons and Gerald M. Platt, *The American University* (Cambridge: Harvard Univ. Press, 1973), ch. 3; Joseph Ben-David, "The Profession of Science and Its Powers," *Minerva* 10 (July 1972): 362-383.

13. Everett C. Hughes, "Professions," *Daedalus,* Fall 1963, p. 656; cf. his *Men and Their Work* (Glencoe: Free Press, 1958), esp. ch. 6, "License and Mandate."

14. Most do little or no research, at least little that results in publication. Everett C. Ladd, Jr., and Seymour Martin Lipset, "How Professors Spend Their Time," *Chronicle of Higher Education,* 14 October 1975, p. 2: "Most academics think of themselves as 'teachers' and 'professionals,' not as 'scholars' and 'intellectuals'— and they perform accordingly. . . . faculty members are producing a prodigious volume of printed words, [but] this torrent is gushing forth from relatively few pens."

15. Ben-David, "The Profession of Science and Its Powers," p. 381: "It is clear that the self-regulating arrangements of the scientific community cannot offer guidance

for decisions regarding the total outlay of funds for science. . . . Such a decision far exceeds the jurisdiction and competence of the self-regulatory mechanisms of the scientific community. The attempt of the scientific community to monopolize social decisions about science might, therefore, in the end be as self-defeating as the attempts of the priesthoods of great religions to control the course of religious sensibility and religious beliefs." Ben-David is surely right, but we can go much further. Not only can science not control social decisions about science, such as how much money should be spent in support of research; it cannot control the social decision over what constitutes science, that is, what kinds of inquiry are to be recognized as having trustworthy results about real objects of inquiry. But this is not to deny that what new groups get recognized depends heavily on the judgment of the already recognized groups.

16. "If one is looking for a date of passing the watershed . . . one might seize on 1946, with the passage of the Full Employment Act creating the Council of Economic Advisers and the Joint Economic Committee in Congress. This represented, as it were, the legitimation of economics as a profession and the establishment of economists as 'lords spiritual' in the precincts of both the White House and Congress" (Kenneth E. Boulding, *The Impact of the Social Sciences* [New Brunswick, N.J.: Rutgers Univ. Press, 1966], p. 38).

17. "Making a discriminating selection of data, as was done in preparing the *International Critical Tables,* requires scientific insight of high order, and is itself an essential scientific activity" (*Science, Government, and Information,* p. 33). "In these four lectures . . . we find the simplicity and modesty of tone which is the prerogative of those who are completely in command of their subject and are thus best able to tell what in the present state of knowledge are the limits of our information, where further investigations are called for, and which of our conclusions still remain hypothetical" (Jean Starobinski, review of Owsei Temkin, *Galenism, New York Review of Books,* 26 June 1975, p. 15).

18. See Michael Polanyi, "The Republic of Science: Its Political and Economic Theory," *Minerva* 1 (Autumn 1962): 54-73, repr. in Edward Shils, ed., *Criteria for Scientific Development: Public Policy and National Goals, A Selection of Articles from Minerva* (Cambridge: M.I.T. Press, 1968).

19. This is the view of Felix Kaufmann, *Methodology of the Social Sciences* (London: Oxford Univ. Press, 1944).

20. See the deservedly well-known work of Thomas Kuhn, *The Structure of Scientific Revolutions,* 2d ed., enlarged (Chicago: Univ. of Chicago Press, 1970); and Margaret Masterman, "The Nature of a Paradigm," in Imre Lakatos and Alan Musgrave, eds., *Criticism and the Growth of Knowledge* (Cambridge: Cambridge University Press, 1970), pp. 59-89. (The whole volume is on Kuhn's work.)

21. Ziman's account of science as public knowledge (in his *Public Knowledge*) appears to require this.

22. Stephen Toulmin, *Human Understanding* (Princeton: Princeton Univ. Press, 1972), vol. 1, p. 264: "When we say, 'It is known that so-and-so,' or 'Biochemistry tells us that so-and-so,' therefore, we do not mean that everyone knows, or that every biochemist will tell us that so-and-so. We normally imply, rather, that this is

the 'authoritative' view: both in the disciplinary sense, i.e. the view supported by the best accredited body of experience, and also in the professional sense, i.e. the view supported by the influential authorities in the subject." Cole and Cole, *Social Stratification in Science,* pp. 78-79: "Scientific progress is in part dependent upon maintaining consensus by vesting intellectual authority in stars. Without consensus, scientists would go off in hundreds of different directions, and science might lose its cumulative character. The stars in a particular field determine which ideas are acceptable and which are not. Abandoning the principle of authority would eliminate a rational basis for discarding poor or irrelevant work." The Coles confuse influence, which certainly is very unequally distributed, with authority to decide what is and what is not to be believed. It is surprising to hear that, without such authority, there would be no rational basis for discarding poor or irrelevant work.

23. Feyerabend (" 'Science,' The Myth and Its Role in Society," pp. 169-170) argues that "no scientist will admit that voting plays a role in his subject," but that "a more detailed analysis of successful moves in the game of science shows indeed that there is a wide range of freedom that permits the application of democratic procedures (ballot-discussion-vote) but which is actually closed by power politics and propaganda."

24. Jacques Barzun, "Notes on the Making of a World Encyclopedia," *American Behavioral Scientist* 6 (Sept. 1962): 8.

25. Cf. George Sarton's discussion of real and potential knowledge, in *The Study of the History of Science* (New York: Dover, © 1936), pp. 31-32 (bound with his *The Study of the History of Mathematics*).

26. There are handbooks, and then there are *Handbuecher;* on the latter, see K.-Chr. Buschbeck, W. Lippert, and E. Uehlein, "Das systematische Handbuch in der naturwissenschaftlichen Literatur," *Naturwissenschaften* 55 (1968): 379-384.

27. See Harvey Einbinder, *The Myth of the Britannica* (New York: Grove Press, 1964); also Samuel McCracken, "The Scandal of 'Britannica 3,' " *Commentary,* February 1976, pp. 63-68. I wish all reference librarians (and their professional school instructors) would read Oskar Morgenstern, *On the Accuracy of Economic Observations,* 2d ed. (Princeton: Princeton Univ. Press, 1963), to learn about the accuracy of the official statistical publications they use as sources of answers to reference questions.

28. *Science, Government, and Information,* pp. 32-33; see also Weisman, *Information Systems, Services, and Centers;* and, not only on information analysis centers but on the whole of the subject matter of this section, National Academy of Sciences—National Academy of Engineering, Committee on Scientific and Technical Communication, *Scientific and Technical Communication: A Pressing National Problem and Recommendations for Its Solution,* National Academy of Sciences Publication 1707 (Washington, D.C., 1969), ch. 6, "Consolidation and Reprocessing—Services for the User."

29. David Garvin, "The Information Analysis Center and the Library," *Special Libraries* 62 (Jan. 1971): 17-23.

30. H. G. Wells, *World Brain* (Garden City: Doubleday, Doran, 1938), pp. 70-71.

31. See, for instance, *Critical Evaluation of Data in the Physical Sciences—*

A Status Report on the National Standard Reference Data System, June 1970,
National Bureau of Standards Technical Note 553 (Washington, D.C., 1970).

32. Wells, *World Brain*, p. 69.

33. The differences among systems serving practitioners that are discipline-,
field-, and problem-oriented (three orientations corresponding reasonably well
to our three bases of organization of reference works) are discussed in William
Paisley's "Improving a Field-Based 'Eric-Like' Information System" *Journal of the
American Society for Information Science* 22 (Nov.-Dec. 1971): 399-408.

34. Herbert Warren Wind, "The House of Baedeker," *New Yorker*, 22 Sept.
1975, pp. 42-93.

35. National Science Board, Special Commission on the Social Sciences, *Knowledge into Action: Improving the Nation's Use of the Social Sciences* (Washington,
D.C.: National Science Foundation, 1969), p. xiii: "The professions are among the
main institutions through which social science knowledge can be translated into
day-to-day knowledge. . . . Professional schools should include in their curricula
more of the social science knowledge relevant to the particular profession."

36. Paul Dickson, *Think Tanks* (New York: Atheneum, 1971), p. 28: "The
primary function of a think tank as the term is used here is neither traditional basic
research, applied research, or development . . . but to act as a bridge between knowledge and power and between science/technology and policy-making in areas of
broad interest. They are closer to being agents of new knowledge and discovery
than creators of new knowledge."

37. Yehezkel Dror, *Design for Policy Sciences* (New York: American Elsevier,
1971), p. 7: " . . . the output of behavioral sciences in terms of explicit policy-
relevant knowledge is hard to pin down. . . . One can go through one behavioral
sciences book after another without being able to identify more than a handful of
policy-relevant items." And on the report cited above in note 35, Dror remarks:
"The Commission clearly tried hard to prove the importance of the behavioral
sciences for social problems and action. Nevertheless, the report is not at all convincing to someone who is not convinced in advance. This is an exact reflection
of reality and not of any lack of effort on the part of the Commission" (p. 7).
A similar point about behavioral science is made in Henry M. Hart, Jr., and John T.
McNaughton, "Evidence and Inference in the Law," in *Evidence and Inference,*
ed. by Daniel Lerner (Glencoe: Free Press, 1959), p. 67.

CHAPTER 2

1. While there is a good deal of descriptive material on individual information
gathering, there is not much theory, except in the literature of statistical decision
theory, which is normative rather than empirical. Some of the most important work
on the theory of information-gathering behavior is that of Anthony Downs, especially
An Economic Theory of Democracy (New York: Harper & Row, 1957), pt. 3:
"Specific Effects of Information Costs," an analysis of "the economics of becoming

informed," and his *Inside Bureaucracy* (Boston: Little, Brown, 1967), chs. 14-16. In the former work, Downs discusses the creation of individual systems of information acquisition; our discussion parallels his in many particulars (though he does not make our distinctions between monitor and reserve system, concerns and interests, and costly ignorance and knowledge) and, where it diverges, is (I think) compatible with his, which has a different orientation (specifically, to political decision). Downs leans more heavily than seems to me quite right on the *free* supply of information; this can be misleading unless one recalls that he means "free of money costs." He stresses the costs of time and effort as much as we do. His discussion of delegation of analysis and evaluation is particularly important (pp. 230-234). His discussion of the decision to acquire an additional bit of information (in terms of expected pay-off, pp. 214-247) is unlike our more general and less detailed account in this and the next chapter. In *Inside Bureaucracy,* the focus is on bureaucratic decision making; the notion of the performance gap appears (cf. our discussion in the section entitled "How Much Is Enough?" pp. 68-73), but in terms of particular decisions rather than overall performance (i.e., the recognition of a performance gap leads to the attempt to find a single course of action that will close the gap) (pp. 169-170).

Of theoretical work in mass communication research, the work that is most closely related to this chapter is Charles Atkin, "Instrumental Utilities and Information Seeking," ch. 7 in *New Models for Mass Communication Research*, ed. Peter Clarke, Sage Annual Reviews of Communication Research, vol. 2 (Beverly Hills: Sage Publications, 1973), pp. 205-242. Atkin summarizes much other research that bears on the subject of this chapter and that is in general consistent with our own generalizations. Atkin's own model is based on different types of uncertainty, which is fine for particular decisions but not quite so fine for determination of a level of information gathering regularly, which is what is of prime interest here. But his model is consistent with our own.

Organizational information systems (for instance, marketing information systems and management information systems) can be considered as counterparts to the personal information systems that concern us; an organizational information system used by a particular individual would be a part or component of that individual's personal information system. See Philip Kotler, *Marketing Management: Analysis, Planning, and Control,* 2d ed. (Englewood Cliffs, N.J.: Prentice-Hall, 1972), ch. 10, for a good description of marketing information systems.

Information on the content and file structure of a number of personal document collections in the area of natural resources research is given in Hilary DePace Burton, *Personal Documentation Methods and Practices, with Analysis of Their Relation to Formal Bibliographic Systems and Theory* (Ph.D. dissertation, University of California, Berkeley, 1972). My own interest in the subject of this chapter was stimulated by Dr. Burton's work, done under supervision of a committee of which I was chairman.

William D. Garvey and Belver C. Griffith, "Scientific Communication as a Social System," *Science* 157 (1 Sept. 1967): 1011-1016, stress the systematic information-seeking behavior of individual scientists as responsible for the "impressively lawful features" of the scientific communication system as a whole. Our interest is in individual behavior rather than in the social system of communication, and we are arguing the hypothesis of the existence of discoverable regularities in individual behavior generally, though we are not claiming that everyone behaves in the same way.

Compare Wilbur Schramm, "The Nature of Communication Between Humans," in Schramm and Donald F. Roberts, *The Process and Effects of Mass Communication*, rev. ed. (Urbana: Univ. of Illinois Press, 1971), pp. 32-33, where, despite an insistence on the large part played by accident, Schramm comes close to recognizing the patterns that we are considering information systems.

2. See the valuable work of Wilbur Schramm and Serena Wade, *Knowledge and the Public Mind: A Preliminary Study of the Distribution and Sources of Science, Health, and Public Affairs Knowledge in the American Public* (Stanford: Institute for Communication Research, Stanford University, 1967) (ERIC Report ED 030 327), pp. 63 and 98. The whole work is highly relevant to this chapter. Schramm and Wade stress what is also discussed in many other sources, that the amount of formal education is the best predictor of the amount of information a person is likely to have, that one's pattern of media use predicts the source(s) of the information, and that a number of personal variables—role, sex, and particularly occupation—will predict the kind of information gathered.

3. "Gossip, that prime leisure activity of the time, played a vital role in a milieu where many, through lack of education, relied entirely on the spoken word. . . . that daily feature of the slum scene, the 'hen party,' did not function, as many thought, merely to peddle scandal; matrons in converse were both storing and redistributing information that could be important economically to themselves and their neighbours" (Robert Roberts, *The Classic Slum: Salford Life in the First Quarter of the Century* [Harmondsworth: Penguin Books, 1973], p. 43).

4. Edwin B. Parker and William J. Paisley, *Patterns of Adult Information Seeking* (Stanford: Stanford University, 1966) (ERIC Report ED 010 294), vol. 3, pp. 43-45, report some data on adult use of "specific types of reference books" which would count as reserve sources if the works used were specifically known in advance of use and not discovered by a special search. Parker and Paisley's work is a mine of information on the information-seeking behavior of adults in two California cities, San Mateo and Fresno. I would not think it safe to generalize from findings about the inhabitants of San Mateo, a rich community of mostly professional people.

5. Indications of such plans can be got by posing hypothetical questions; see, for instance, the survey conducted for the Public Library Inquiry in 1948: Angus Campbell and Charles A. Metzner, *Public Use of the Library and Other Sources of Information*, rev. ed. (Ann Arbor: Institute for Social Research, Univ. of Michigan, 1952), pp. 12-15, esp. p. 15: "It is clear from the survey that a large proportion of the public feel satisfied with the information they obtain from newspapers and radio and do not seek further for additional material, at least as far as knowledge of world affairs is concerned." That would be what Downs (see n. 1 above) calls free information (but newspapers are not free). See also Brenda Dervin and Bradley S. Greenberg, "The Communication Environment of the Urban Poor," ch. 7 in *Current Perspectives in*

Mass Communication Research, ed. F. Gerald Kline and Phillip J. Tichenor, Sage Annual Reviews of Communication Research, vol. 1 (Beverly Hills: Sage Publications, 1972); they argue that ghetto residents are prepared to consult "establishment" sources of information, advice, and help in time of crisis, and that for crisis problems, such as finding a job or helping a friend under arrest, "very specific establishment sources are well known and sought out," even though they are mistrusted as exploiters.

6. Robert D. Leigh, *The Public Library in the United States* (New York: Columbia Univ. Press, 1950), p. 49: "Fortunately, the democratic process does not require a universal, equal acceptance of the burden of obtaining and digesting information and weighing ideas on current affairs. In the face of the impossible task of examining all the material and all the issues, most of us voluntarily delegate analysis and leadership in making decisions to people whom we trust. We choose these people freely, and we change our choices at will." Also see n. 1 above.

7. There is abundant evidence for this preference among scientific and technical people. See the superb review by William J. Paisley, *The Flow of (Behavioral) Science Information: A Review of the Research Literature* (Stanford: Institute for Communication Research, Stanford University, 1965) (ERIC Report ED 039 783). The preference for personal over impersonal sources, especially over print sources (as against television, for instance), is stressed in Dervin and Greenberg, "The Communication Environment of the Urban Poor," as in many other sources on the lives of the urban and rural poor. The same preference appears among the best and the worst educated, then.

8. An earlier attempt at this distinction was made in my "Situational Relevance," *Information Storage and Retrieval* 9 (1973): 457-471.

9. Everett C. Ladd, Jr., and Seymour Martin Lipset found that "the more faculty members try to influence the course of events in the university and the society, the more they read journals of social, political, economic, and cultural commentary. . . . The general conclusion that readers are activists is sustained not only for the entire range of periodicals examined, but for every subgroup within the list. . . . Faculty members who read most widely among general periodicals are led to do so not by some special measure of intellectuality, as we had expected, but rather by a special interest in doing things to influence the flow of decisions and events" (*Chronicle of Higher Education,* 19 January 1976, p. 14). This factor of activism—which, together with academic discipline and ideology, "together pretty much explain journal readership among faculty members"—is a measure of what we call concern; the higher the degree of concern, the more one tends to read in the areas of one's concern. This is what one would expect, but it is nice to have confirmation from Ladd and Lipset.

10. See Hadley Cantril, *The Pattern of Human Concerns* (New Brunswick, N.J.: Rutgers Univ. Press, 1965), an international survey of hopes and fears. Cantril's use of *concern* is not the same as ours but in practice is about equivalent.

11. See Alfred Schutz, "The Well-Informed Citizen," in his *Collected Papers II: Studies in Social Theory,* Phaenomenologica 15 (The Hague: Nijhoff, 1964), pp. 120-134, perhaps the best introduction to Schutz's important work on relevance. The relevance we are speaking of is what he called "intrinsic relevance" (p. 126).

The "man on the street . . . does not even look for any kind of information that goes beyond his habitual system of intrinsic relevances" (p. 134). This essay of Schutz is offered as a contribution to "a theoretical science dealing with the social distribution of knowledge," a science that unfortunately has not advanced much beyond his own work. The best general introduction to the sociology of knowledge is Peter L. Berger and Thomas Luckmann, *The Social Construction of Reality: A Treatise in the Sociology of Knowledge* (Garden City, N.J.: Doubleday, Anchor Books A589, 1967). See also Kurt H. Wolff, "The Sociology of Knowledge in the United States of America: A Trend Report and Bibliography, *Current Sociology* 15, no. 1 (1967). The classic in the field is Karl Mannheim, *Ideology and Utopia: An Introduction to the Sociology of Knowledge,* trans. by Louis Wirth and Edward Shils (London: Kegan Paul, 1936).

12. James Boswell, *Life of Johnson* (18 April 1775) (New York: Oxford Univ. Press, 1948), vol. 1, p. 595.

13. See Schramm and Wade, *Knowledge and the Public Mind,* and, for another secondary analysis of existing sample surveys, Herbert H. Hyman, Charles R. Wright, and John Shelton Reed, *The Enduring Effects of Education* (Chicago: University of Chicago Press, 1975).

14. In particular, relations of dominance and subordination, of giving and taking orders, would give rise to a hierarchical structure; this is the occupational structure of concern to Samuel Bowles and Herbert Gintis, *Schooling in Capitalist America* (New York: Basic Books, 1976), a powerful analysis of the relationship of educational system to occupational structure.

15. Amount of formal education correlates highly with social prestige, but less highly, if we are right about farmers and craftsmen and foremen, with amount of knowledge needed and used in one's work. That should not be surprising; much of formal education is not meant to serve a practical purpose. But in that case, educational credentials required for employment become suspect. See Ivar Berg, *Education and Jobs: The Great Training Robbery* (Boston: Beacon Press, 1971).

16. U.S. Dept. of Labor, *Dictionary of Occupational Titles,* 2 vols., 3d ed. (Washington, D.C.: Government Printing Office, 1965).

17. The social centrality of occupation is widely recognized, as in Peter M. Blau and Otis Dudley Duncan, *The American Occupational Structure* (New York: Wiley, 1967), pp. 6-7: "The occupational structure in modern industrial society not only constitutes an important foundation for the main dimensions of social stratification but also serves as the connecting link between different institutions and spheres of social life, and therein lies its great significance. The hierarchy of prestige strata and the hierarchy of economic classes have their roots in the occupational structure; so does the hierarchy of political power and authority, for political authority in modern society is largely exercised as a full-time occupation. . . . The occupational structure is also the link between the economy and the family, through which the economy affects the family's status and the family supplies manpower to the economy. The hierarchy of occupational strata reveals the relationship between the social contributions men make by furnishing various services and the rewards they receive in return, whether or not this relationship expresses some equitable

functional adjustment." Also see Ralf Dahrendorf, *Class and Class Conflict in Industrial Society* (Stanford: Stanford Univ. Press, 1959), p. 70: "Whatever criterion of social stratification one prefers, prestige or income, spending habits or styles of life, education or independence, they all lead back to occupation." But see pp. 272-274 for discussion of the claim that the centrality of occupation is diminishing. On the interests of people at different occupational and social strata, explicitly discussed in terms of information gathering, see Joffre Dumazedier, *Toward a Society of Leisure* (New York: Free Press, 1967), ch. 10, "Leisure, Education, and the Masses," which I discovered too late to use fully in this work.

18. Karl Marx and Friedrich Engels, *The German Ideology, Part One,* ed. by C. J. Arthur (New York: International Publishers, 1970), p. 53.

19. These figures are from Alexander Szalai, ed., *The Use of Time: Daily Activities of Urban and Suburban Populations in Twelve Countries,* Publications of the European Centre for Research and Documentation in the Social Sciences 5 (The Hague: Mouton, 1972), ch. 6, "Everyday Life in Twelve Countries." In this vast survey (over 30,000 respondents), only working-age adults were studied; those under 18 and over 65 were excluded. These international averages contrast sharply with figures on media use among the urban poor in the United States given by Dervin and Greenberg, "The Communication Environment of the Urban Poor," p. 201; Dervin and Greenberg report that the average low-income adult spends almost eight hours a day on electronic media. For a fascinating study of the use of time by an economist, see Staffan Burenstam Linder, *The Harried Leisure Class* (New York: Columbia Univ. Press, 1970), especially ch. 6, "The Rationale of Growing Irrationality," on information costs, and ch. 8, "Culture Time."

20. Szalai, *The Use of Time,* p. 187. Gary A. Steiner (*The People Look at Television: A Study of Audience Attitudes* [New York: Knopf, 1963], p. 229) notes how little television is used for information or education: "Aside from the day's news and weather—which he (the average American viewer) watches regularly—he rarely uses the set as a deliberate source of information, and he is extremely unlikely to turn on serious and informative public affairs presentations, even if he is watching while they are on the air."

21. See Machlup, *The Production and Distribution of Knowledge in the United States,* ch. 7, "Information Services."

22. "As people learn more, their interest increases, and as their interest increases they are impelled to learn more" (Herbert H. Hyman and Paul B. Sheatsley, "Some Reasons Why Information Campaigns Fail," *Public Opinion Quarterly* 11 [1947]: 416). "Persons who are already better informed are likely to be aware of a topic when it appears in the mass media and are better prepared to understand it" (P. J. Tichenor et al., "Mass Media Flow and Differential Growth in Knowledge," *Public Opinion Quarterly* 34 [1970]: 162). This and further related factors led Tichenor and his colleagues to suggest a "knowledge gap," an increasingly uneven distribution of knowledge.

23. Cf. Downs, *An Economic Theory of Democracy,* p. 210, on transferable and nontransferable costs.

24. I am ignoring the problem of information overload, but not because I do

not think it a real problem for many people. I am inclined to think it is often what might be called a moral problem: one has more information than one has time or ability to master and apply, or one thinks that there exists somewhere more information than one would be able to master and apply; so one makes decisions in which, one thinks, information that one ought to be taking into account is being left out of account. One response is simply to try to change one's view of what is required, for it cannot be required to do the impossible. I agree with Herbert Simon ("Designing Organizations for an Information-Rich World," in Martin Greenberger, ed., *Computers, Communications, and the Public Interest* [Baltimore: Johns Hopkins Press, 1971], p. 72): "The information overload is in the mind of the reader. Information does not have to be processed just because it is there. Filtering by intelligent programs is the main part of the answer." But this requires not only that one find a way of filtering (or forgetting), but also that one convince oneself that it is all right to filter (or forget). And this may entail a change in one's moral attitude to the use of information in decision making. An easier sort of information overload is that which consists simply of too much irrelevant information: there is no moral problem there, just an organizational one.

25. Empirical confirmation is surveyed in David O. Sears and Jonathan L. Freedman, "Selective Exposure to Information: A Critical Review," *Public Opinion Quarterly* 31 (1967): 194-213 (repr. in Schramm and Roberts, *The Process and Effects of Mass Communication*, pp. 209-234).

26. See Olaf Helmer and Nicholas Rescher, "On the Epistemology of the Inexact Sciences," *Management Science* 6 (Oct. 1959): 25-52; Michael Polanyi, *Personal Knowledge: Towards A Post-Critical Philosophy* (New York: Harper & Row, Harper Torchbooks, 1964).

27. One must be skeptical of accounts of losses due to ignorance. There is a great deal of folklore on the topic. See Anthony G. Oettinger, "An Essay in Information Retrieval, or, The Birth of a Myth," *Information and Control* 8 (1965): 64-79 (reviewed in *Mathematical Reviews* 29 [1965], entry no. 6960). But also see C. W. Hanson, "Research on Users' Needs: Where Is It Getting Us?" *Aslib Proceedings* 16 (Feb. 1964): p. 71: "Some six hundred research scientists gave us details of literature they had discovered which, had it been found earlier, would have caused them to alter their research in some way, or would have saved them time or money. Of 238 such cases, in only three, just over 1 per cent, was the document drawn to their attention by library staff. None were discovered via the library card index. The researchers were much more indebted to other people (33 per cent), to cited references (18 per cent), and to chance (16 per cent)."

28. See J. M. Brittain, *Information and Its Users: A Review with Special Reference to the Social Sciences* (Bath: Bath Univ. Press, 1970), pp. 1-2; Maurice B. Line, "Draft Definitions: Information and Library Needs, Wants, Demands and Uses," *Aslib Proceedings* 26 (Feb. 1974): 87 (*need* is defined as "what an individual *ought* to have, for his work, his research, his edification, his recreation, etc."); John O'Connor, "Some Questions Concerning 'Information Need,'" *American Documentation* 19 (Apr. 1968): 200-203; Thomas Childers, *The Information-Poor in America* (Metuchen, N.J.: Scarecrow, 1975), pp. 14-16, 35-38.

29. As far as I am aware, all serious attempts to define measures of the value of information assume that these conditions hold. See, for instance, Russell L. Ackoff, "Towards a Behavioral Theory of Communication," *Management Science* 4 (1958): 218-234.

30. The notion of an acceptable decision situation is closely related to Herbert A. Simon's notion of satisficing; see his *Models of Man, Social and Rational* (New York: John Wiley, 1957), especially ch. 14, "A Behavioral Model of Rational Choice" (reprinted from *Quarterly Journal of Economics* 69 [1955] : 129-138), and pp. 204-205: "The key to the simplification of the choice process . . . is the replacement of the goal of maximizing with the goal of satisficing, of finding a course of action that is 'good enough' " rather than trying to find the best possible course of action.

31. The difference between seeking information and seeking education can be made in this way (no doubt there are others): seeking information is seeking what fits into already established conceptual structures, while seeking education is seeking to add new structures or revise old ones. In this sense, much of what is called "education" would not deserve the name; learning new facts of familiar sorts is not education. The same sources may provide both information and education, of course.

32. A large and highly technical literature deals with what might be called the theory of further inquiry: the problem of deciding when it is worthwhile to acquire further information. Perhaps the best moderately easy introduction is Howard Raiffa, *Decision Analysis: Introductory Lectures on Choices Under Uncertainty* (Reading, Mass.: Addison-Wesley, 1968).

33. As costly knowledge leads to making worse decisions, information or advice got by a special search may make a decision situation worse rather than better; on this point, see, for instance, Harry Nyström, "Uncertainty, Information and Organizational Decision-Making: A Cognitive Approach," *Swedish Journal of Economics*, 1974, pp. 131-139, and Bruce J. Whittemore and M. C. Yovits, "A Generalized Conceptual Development for the Analysis and Flow of Information," *Journal of the American Society for Information Science* 24 (May-June 1973): 221-231.

34. I am not counting the credibility of a source as a separate factor in evaluation or source selection, since a judgment that a source is productive of information implies credibility; when we judge a source productive of information, that judgment carries an evaluation that we are getting information, not misinformation But this is only a minor economy, and it would be perfectly reasonable to count estimates of credibility in as selection factors.

35. See Steven H. Chaffee and Jack M. McLeod, "Individual vs. Social Predictors of Information Seeking," *Journalism Quarterly* 50 (Summer 1973): 237-245, on information gathered on the basis of its anticipated social utility. Of course, showing off *is* making use of the information one shows off, and if we collect information to have something to talk about with others, we are collecting with future use in mind. But the use is still an odd one that does not fit comfortably in the same category with use in decision making.

36. On changes in communication behavior at different points of the life cycle, see Jack M. McLeod and Garrett J. O'Keefe, Jr., "The Socialization Perspective and Communication Behavior," *Current Perspectives in Mass Communication Research,*

ed. F. Gerald Kline and Phillip J. Tichenor, Sage Annual Reviews of Communication Research, vol. 1 (Beverly Hills, 1972), pp. 121-168. On changes in information correlated with age, see Schramm and Wade, *Knowledge and the Public Mind.*

37. On the effects of war on newspaper reading habits in Great Britain and the U.S., see Colin Cherry, *World Communication: Threat or Promise? A Socio-Technical Approach* (London: Wiley, 1971), pp. 195-196.

38. "Any reorganization of work that moves the practice of a profession from a private unobserved activity to one that receives regular surveillance from other professionals is likely to put a premium on the possession of current knowledge and skills" (John K. Folger, Helen S. Astin, and Alan E. Bayer, *Human Resources and Higher Education, Staff Report of the Commission on Human Resources and Advanced Education* [New York: Russell Sage Foundation, 1970], p. 366). The scrutiny of colleagues from the same profession is not the only thing that can put pressure on people to keep up to date and perform effectively; threats of malpractice suits should be quite effective. "Virtually anyone who serves the general public and professes to have a special knowledge or skill is vulnerable to claims of professional or quasi-professional neglect . . . . consumer protection and legal rights occupy centerstage in the legal theater" (anonymous quotation in *San Francisco Chronicle,* 5 November 1975).

39. See Amos Tversky and Daniel Kahneman, "Judgment Under Uncertainty: Heuristics and Biases," *Science* 185 (27 Sept. 1974): 1124-1131.

40. Information-gathering style is just one aspect of more general managerial style, of great importance to those concerned with management information systems; see C. West Churchman, "What Is Information for Policy Making?" in Manfred Kochen, ed., *Information for Action: From Knowledge to Wisdom* (New York: Academic Press, 1975), pp. 33-40, and Kottler, *Marketing Management,* ch. 10.

41. See Donald F. Cox and Robert E. Good, "How to Build a Marketing Information System," *Harvard Business Review,* May-June 1967, p. 152: " . . . what happens when only the level of information quality is raised significantly? Our prediction is that this would not lead to better decisions. In fact, the reverse may be true, as the result of the confusion and resentment generated by the manager's inability to deal with the more sophisticated information." Also see n. 33 above. Compare Warren F. Ilchman and Norman Thomas Uphoff, *The Political Economy of Change* (Berkeley: Univ. of California Press, 1971), pp. 260-262: "We would propose that social scientists should proceed on the assumption that some optimal amount of ignorance exists on any particular subject. . . . Acceptance of the notion of optimal ignorance signifies a consciousness of the costs of augmenting knowledge." On the same concept, see Guy Benveniste, *The Politics of Expertise* (Berkeley: Glendessary Press, 1972), pp. 176-177. Against optimal ignorance, however, is a strong tradition in favor of the "requirement of total evidence"; see Rudolf Carnap, *Logical Foundations of Probability* (London: Routledge, 1950), pp. 211-213. The issue is one of great depth, but until recently, I think, "total evidence" has been without serious challenge as the proper ideal. "Optimal ignorance" sounds wicked.

42. This raises the question of selective exposure to information, which has been of major interest in communication research; see Sears and Freedman, "Selective

Exposure to Information," and Lewis Donohew and Leonard Tipton, "A Conceptual Model of Information Seeking, Avoiding, and Processing," ch. 8 in Peter Clarke, ed., *New Models for Mass Communication Research,* Sage Annual Reviews of Communication Research, vol. 2 (Beverly Hills: Sage Publications, 1973), pp. 243-268. But I think that the question has not been exhausted.

CHAPTER 3

1. See James M. Buchanan, *The Demand and Supply of Public Goods* (Chicago: Rand McNally, 1968).

2. See Burton A. Weisbrod, "Collective-Consumption Services of Individual-Consumption Goods," *Quarterly Journal of Economics* 78 (Aug. 1964): 471-477.

3. On the frequency of use of public and other sorts of libraries, see *Libraries at Large,* ed. Douglas M. Knight and E. Shepley Nourse (New York: Bowker, 1969), ch. 2, and the still indispensable Bernard Berelson, *The Library's Public* (New York: Columbia Univ. Press, 1949). See also *The Role of Libraries in America: A Report of the Survey Conducted by The Gallup Organization, Inc., for the Chief Officers of State Library Agencies* (Frankfort: Kentucky Department of Library and Archives, 1976). On studies of library use in general: Leon Carnovsky, "Survey of the Use of Library Resources and Facilities," in *Library Surveys,* ed. by Maurice F. Tauber and Irlene Roemer Stephens, Columbia University Studies in Library Service 16 (New York: Columbia Univ. Press, 1967), pp. 71-89.

4. On the relative proportions of "known-title" searches, see: *Catalog Use Study,* Director's Report by Sidney L. Jackson (Chicago: American Library Association, 1958); Richard P. Palmer, *Computerizing the Card Catalog in the University Library: A Survey of User Requirements,* Research Studies in Library Science, no. 6 (Littleton, Colo.: Libraries Unlimited, 1972).

5. Cf. "Mooer's Law: An information retrieval system will tend *not* to be used whenever it is more painful and troublesome for a customer to have information than for him not to have it" (*American Documentation* 11 [July 1960], p. ii). Presumably *get* is meant rather than *have.*

6. There are probably limits on the length of documents one is willing to use, too; the argument here is that there can be an independent limit on the number of different documents one is willing to use together.

7. So the objective of the American Library Association to provide "leadership for inter-library cooperation leading to a nationwide information delivery system which equalizes access to information resources" (ALA press release, January 1975), even if reached, would hardly represent utopia. (The term "access" in the statement of the objective is presumably to be understood in the sense of *availability.*)

8. See Claire K. Lipsman, *The Disadvantaged and Library Effectiveness* (Chicago: American Library Association, 1972), p. 139: "It appears that the only groups for whom the utilization of hard-cover books continues to be necessary in everyday life or serves as an important source of status and satisfaction are motivated students

and highly educated adults. In the urban ghettos there are few of the former and virtually none of the latter."

9. See Philip Morse, *On Browsing: The Use of Search Theory in the Search for Information,* Technical Report no. 50, Operations Research Center, Massachusetts Institute of Technology (Cambridge, 1970), p. 15: "simple roaming through the stacks, which has always been (and *may* always be) the usual way of finding what book one wants." For an extensive discussion and survey of discussions of browsing, see Richard Hyman, *Access to Library Collections* (Metuchen, N.J.: Scarecrow Press, 1972).

10. Roughly the same point is made by Lowell Martin, "Role and Structure of Metropolitan Libraries," in Ralph W. Conant and Kathleen Molz, eds., *The Metropolitan Library* (Cambridge, Mass.: MIT Press, 1972), p. 175.

11. On the need for a library system to compensate for the inadequacies of the retail book business, see Dan Lacy, *Freedom and Communications,* 2d ed. (Urbana: Univ. of Illinois Press, 1965). Cf. John P. Dessauer, *Book Publishing: What It Is, What It Does* (New York: Bowker, 1974).

12. See E. Bright Wilson, Jr., *An Introduction to Scientific Research* (New York: McGraw-Hill, 1952), ch. 2, "Searching the Literature."

13. National Research Council, Division of Behavioral Sciences, Committee on Information in the Behavioral Sciences, *Communication Systems and Resources in the Behavioral Sciences,* National Academy of Sciences Publication 1575 (Washington, D.C., 1967), p. 43. Cf. J. D. Bernal, "Scientific Information and Its Users," *Aslib Proceedings* 12 (Dec. 1960): 432-438, for a scientist's comments on what the literature is good for. See also Christopher Scott, "Technical Information in Industry: How It Is Used," *Aslib Proceedings* 11 (Dec. 1959): 318-326; this particularly interesting report of a survey of the use of technical information in the British electrical and electronics industry argues that the main use of technical literature is as a source of stimulation. Little literature search is reported. On the frequency of extensive searches, see C. W. Hanson, "Research on Users' Needs: Where Is It Getting Us?" *Aslib Proceedings* 16 (1964): 68, 76.

14. For useful bits of evidence on the information-gathering behavior of teachers and professional practitioners, see *Investigation into Information Requirements of the Social Sciences, Research Report No. 3, Information Requirements of College of Education Lecturers and Schoolteachers,* and *Research Report No. 4, The Information Needs of Social Workers* (Bath: Bath Univ. Library, 1971).

15. The contrast between the careful way in which information is dealt with in the area of one's occupational responsibilities and the casual way in which it is treated outside those areas is stressed by Joseph A. Schumpeter in *Capitalism, Socialism and Democracy,* 3d ed. (New York: Harper & Row, Harper Torchbooks, 1962). "We need only compare a lawyer's attitude to his brief and the same lawyer's attitude to the statements of political fact presented in his newspaper in order to see what is the matter. In the one case the lawyer has qualified for appreciating the relevance of his facts by years of purposeful labor done under the definite stimulus of interest in his professional competence; and under a stimulus that is no less powerful he then bends his acquirements, his intellect, his will to the contents of the brief. In the other

case, he has not taken the trouble to qualify; he does not care to absorb the information or to apply to it the canons of criticism he knows so well how to handle; and he is impatient of long or complicated argument. All of this goes to show that without the initiative that comes from immediate responsibility, ignorance will persist in the face of masses of information however complete and correct" (pp. 261-262).

16. This is what Pierce Butler ("Survey of the Reference Field," in *The Reference Function of the Library* [Chicago: Univ. of Chicago Press, 1943], p. 12) calls "pure reference work," in contrast to original investigation, formal education, "social communication" (approximately our monitor system), and "consultation" (asking an expert). " . . . the essence of reference work is not that several books are used at the same time, as is sometimes humorously stated, but that books are used for the sake of their interrelationships with one another in respect to their informative content." This is precisely what those of low studiousness are not prepared to do. Nor, for that matter, do reference librarians often do it.

17. On types of service, the development of service policy, etc., see Samuel Rothstein, *The Development of Reference Services Through Academic Traditions, Public Library Practice and Special Librarianship,* ACRL Monograph no. 14 (Chicago, 1955).

18. Academic libraries pose rather special problems. Students are expected to do their own bibliographical work since it is part of the educational task. Faculty members either do their own, on the ground that no one else can be trusted, or delegate it to students. They might be happy to delegate the more tedious and menial chores to librarians, but would they be willing to delegate, and would librarians be prepared to accept, difficult and also extremely time-consuming jobs? See the section entitled "Some Ideals of Library Service" on library provision of research assistance to research workers.

19. James I. Wyer, *Reference Work: A Textbook for Students of Library Work and Librarians* (Chicago: American Library Association, 1930), p. 116.

20. According to Samuel Rothstein, "The Measurement and Evaluation of Reference Service," *Library Trends* 12 (Jan. 1964): 456-472, most questions asked are directional (half the total) or factual; of the latter, 90 to 95 percent are "ready reference" questions answerable in less than ten minutes, and about half are answered from a very small core of reference works (dictionaries, encyclopedias, and almanacs). Librarians report over 95 percent success, and most customers report satisfaction. Few patrons seek advisory service for personal reading. See also "Reference Service in American Public Libraries Serving Populations of 10,000 or More," University of Illinois Library School Occasional Paper no. 61 (Urbana, 1961) (prepared by Mary Lee Bundy).

21. Lowell A. Martin, *Library Response to Urban Change: A Study of the Chicago Public Library* (Chicago: American Library Association, 1969); Terence Crowley and Thomas Childers, *Information Service in Public Libraries: Two Studies* (Metuchen, N.J.: Scarecrow, 1971); Peat, Marwick, Mitchell & Co., *California Public Library Systems: A Comprehensive Review with Guidelines for the Next Decade* (Los Angeles, 1975).

22. Wyer, *Reference Work*, p. 127.

23. Margaret Hutchins, *Introduction to Reference Work* (Chicago: American Library Association, 1944), pp. 33, 34, 37 (my emphasis).

24. Wyer, *Reference Work*, p. 130.

25. Robert S. Taylor, "Question Negotiation and Information Seeking in Libraries," *College & Research Libraries* 29 (May 1968): 178-194.

26. The alternative is that people ask reference librarians only questions they expect the librarian will be able to answer. The remarks of Robert B. Cronenberger, "Public Library: Library for the People," *RQ* (Summer 1973): 344-345, on neighborhood information centers, support this view: "Studies have occurred in Wisconsin and California indicating that a high percentage of questions to information and referral agencies are requests for pure information. The use of trained social workers to answer information questions has been shown to be wasteful. Most of the questions aimed at an information and referral center are 'Can you give the telephone number of———?' . . . In Detroit's experience to date, there have been almost no questions involving a counseling situation" (p. 345).

27. Mary Lee Bundy and Paul Wasserman, "Professionalism Reconsidered," *College and Research Libraries* 29 (Jan. 1968): 8: "In general library situations, that which is requested by or offered to the patron is ordinarily just not complex enough to be considered a professional service. The service provided would not over-tax the capacity of any reasonably intelligent college graduate after a minimum period of on-the-job training." It is hard to see how one can possibly argue with this. One does not have to be a professional librarian to read sentences and numbers out of ready reference books. But I do not quite see what they propose as the remedy. They speak of the "next stage" in librarians' preparation as the enhancement of subject competence, but to what degree? To full professional competence as a scientist or scholar?

28. As Bundy and Wasserman ("Professionalism Reconsidered") point out, it is the children's librarians who are most "professional," at least in the sense of being most assertive in telling their patrons what they should read. This is easier for them than for other librarians, since they are usually so much larger than their patrons.

29. See note 26 above, and also see Thomas Childers, "The Neighborhood Information Center Project," *Library Quarterly* 46 (July 1976): 271-289. I interpret Childers' discussion of information and referral service objectives in the cities surveyed to mean that the systematic offering of advice is not one of the objectives; as to whether it is asked for, Childers reports, disappointingly, that "very little is known about the nature of the demands on public library I & R services" (p. 287).

30. Jesse H. Shera, *The Foundations of Education for Librarianship* (New York: Becker and Hayes, 1972), p. 194.

31. William S. Learned, *The American Public Library and the Diffusion of Knowledge* (New York: Harcourt, Brace, 1924), pp. 10-16, passim.

32. On change agents, see: Everett M. Rogers, with F. Floyd Shoemaker, *Communication of Innovations: A Cross-Cultural Approach*, 2d ed. (New York: Free Press, 1971), ch. 7; Marshall Sashkind, William C. Morris, and Leslie Horst, "A Comparison of Social and Organizational Change Models: Information Flow and Data Use Processes," *Psychological Review* 80 (1973): 510-526. Schramm and Wade

(*Knowledge and the Public Mind,* pp. 133-134) ask what might be done to raise the level of knowledge in the population at large, and answer: First, raise the level of education, or make it more efficient; second, get more information into the media of mass communication; third, try to make information sources more readily available and easier to use, and try to build up in communities the incentive and practice of seeking and exchanging information.

33. A report on the invitational Conference on User Needs held in Denver in 1973 (National Commission on Libraries and Information Science, *Annual Report, 1972-73,* pp. 26-29) notes that " . . . it seems that society may have to focus on groups rather than on individuals if economically viable information systems are to be created and operated" (p. 28). Since this follows hard on a comment that the television screen is "increasingly favored as a way of gaining access to information," one infers that either (a) new content should be injected into established television programs, or (b) new programs (perhaps on special informational channels?) should be created. The point remains that new programs would compete with old ones.

34. "People wanting to get on welfare do not want the welfare system explained to them, they want to know how to get on welfare. . . . The man going on trial in a domestic case does not want to know the law; he wants to know how to ensure that his case comes before a judge who understands his culture" (Mary Lee Bundy, "Urban Information and Public Libraries: A Design for Service," *Library Journal,* 15 Jan. 1972, p. 166). Bundy's diagnosis is correct, however implausible her prescription. Bundy also makes the point (p. 163) that helping people cope with their situations may divert their attention from changing their situations, a perennial, unavoidable conflict of interest in social life.

35. Learned, *The American Public Library,* p. 15.

36. "Operative technology": Mario Bunge, "Technology as Applied Science," *Technology and Culture* 7 (Summer 1966): 329-347; "intellectual technology": Daniel Bell, *The Coming of Post-Industrial Society* (New York: Basic Books, 1973).

37. "The economic concern, the interest in optimal choices, has of course characterized practical arts such as engineering, military planning, and medicine from their very inception. In our generation, this concern has become articulate. Under names such as operations research, cost-efficiency analysis, systems analysis, mathematical programming—clumsy, casual names suggesting their origin in practice rather than in philosophy—complex decision problems are being stated explicitly as such" (Jacob Marschak and Roy Radner, *Economic Theory of Teams* [New Haven: Yale Univ. Press, 1972], p. 3). "In essence, decision theory can be called the 'economics of information' " (ibid., p. 4), and the applied economics of information becomes a technology of decision.

38. See Joel S. Demski, *Information Analysis* (Reading, Mass.: Addison-Wesley, 1972).

39. See Russell L. Ackoff, "Management Misinformation Systems," *Management Science* 14 (Dec. 1967): B147-156.

40. The potential for improvement of the librarian's slight technology of management of information-bearing objects that is represented by the computer needs no discussion here; it is exhaustively described elsewhere. The enlargement of the library's

stock of reference works by access, via telephone lines, to computer-based files consisting of a current representation of a portion of public knowledge (see ch. 1, "Reference Works" pp. 24-34) is an obvious possibility for improvement of library service.

41. Edwin Parker finds two "fatal flaws" in the claim that information facilities are not wanted and would not be utilized by the economically and culturally deprived segments of American society: first, that the claim ignores the "considerable elasticity of the demand for information," whereby "if society makes education and information resources as freely and easily available to all as television entertainment is now available, utilization of these resources *could* [emphasis added] increase considerably," and, second, that present libraries are "far from free" when "the time and effort required for access by the user is included." But if access time and effort were completely eliminated, reading time and effort would not. Parker goes on: "The only way one can maintain the argument that information would not be used is to assume that information will continue to be as expensive to obtain as it is now or to assume that the information will be irrelevant to the needs and interests of those not now benefiting from existing information resources." But getting information must here mean getting the vehicles of communication (books, or perhaps moving pictures), and providing the vehicles does not make it any easier to come to have for oneself the information they bear. See Edwin B. Parker, "Information and Society," ch. 2 in *Library and Information Service Needs of the Nation: Proceedings of a Conference on the Needs of Occupational, Ethnic, and Other Groups in the United States* (Washington, D.C.: Government Printing Office, 1974, pp. 9-50. A shorter version of this chapter is found in *Annual Review of Information Science and Technology*, vol. 8 (1973), ch. 11.

42. J. Robert Oppenheimer, "Knowledge and the Structure of Culture," The Helen Kenyon Lecture, October 29, 1958 (Poughkeepsie: Vassar College, 1958), pp. 6, 8-9. See Alfred Schutz, "The Well-Informed Citizen," in his *Collected Papers II: Studies in Social Theory*, Phaenomenologica 15 (The Hague: Nijhoff, 1964), p. 120: "The outstanding feature of a man's life in the modern world is his conviction that his life-world as a whole is neither fully understood by him nor fully understandable to any of his fellow-men." The hypothesis of an increasingly uneven distribution of knowledge, a "knowledge gap" between the well and the poorly educated, is discussed by P. J. Tichenor et al., "Mass Media Flow and Differential Growth in Knowledge," *Public Opinion Quarterly* 34 (1970): 159-170. That is not the gap in question here; it is the inevitable ignorance of even the well educated.

43. Following a very different path, we have come to conclusions similar to those reached by Wilhelm Munthe, *American Librarianship from A European Angle* (Chicago: American Library Association, 1939), p. 53, and Robert D. Leigh, *The Public Library in the United States* (New York: Columbia Univ. Press, 1950), end of ch. 3. Both authors stress the indirect benefits to nonusers of libraries of good service to influential minorities.

INDEX

About the Author

Patrick Wilson, professor at the School of Library and Information Studies, University of California, Berkeley, specializes in bibliographical organization and the organization of knowledge. He has written articles for such journals as *Inquiry, Monist, Folia Humanistica,* and *Information Storage and Retrieval.* His previous books include *Government and Politics of India and Pakistan, 1885-1955: A Bibliography of Works in Western Languages* and *Two Kinds of Power: An Essay on Bibliographical Control.*